ONE TEACHER IN TEN
IN THE NEW MILLENNIUM

One Teacher in Ten in the New Millennium

*LGBT Educators Speak Out About
What's Gotten Better . . . and What Hasn't*

EDITED BY KEVIN JENNINGS

Beacon Press
Boston

BEACON PRESS
Boston, Massachusetts
www.beacon.org

Beacon Press books
are published under the auspices of
the Unitarian Universalist Association of Congregations.

Printed in the United States of America

18 17 16 15   8 7 6 5 4 3 2 1

This book is printed on acid-free paper that meets the uncoated paper
ANSI/NISO specifications for permanence as revised in 1992.

Text design and composition by Kim Arney

Library of Congress Cataloging-in-Publication Data
One teacher in ten in the new millennium : LGBT educators speak out about what's
gotten better and what hasn't / edited by Kevin Jennings.
    pages cm
ISBN 978-0-8070-5586-1 (paperback)
ISBN 978-0-8070-5587-8 (ebook)
1. Gay teachers—United States—Biography. 2. Lesbian teachers—United States—
Biography. 3. Bisexual teachers—United States—Biography. 4. Transgender
teachers—United States—Biography. I. Jennings, Kevin—editor.
    LB2844.1.G39O645 2015
    371.100'8664—dc23
                                                              2015000514

For Jeff and for our furry kids

Luke (1999–2000)
Amber (2000–2012)
Ben (2006–2014)
Jackson
Sloane

Contents

Preface

On November 10, 1988, at age twenty-five, I strode to the podium of the chapel at the school where I taught (Concord Academy in Concord, Massachusetts) and gave a fifteen-minute talk in which I came out as gay to my students.

It was a very different time for LGBT people in 1988. Ronald Reagan was president. AIDS, a disease for which no treatment was available, was claiming the lives of tens of thousands of gay men like me. Only one state protected people from being fired because of their sexual orientation, and it wasn't Massachusetts. (Wondering which one? Answer at the end of the book.)

I knew no one who had ever done what I was doing. I had never met an openly LGBT teacher. K–12 schools had no organizations dedicated to LGBT issues. I felt like I was diving off a cliff.

Much of my life has been spent trying to correct the injustices I saw in the schools I attended and in the ones where I taught, injustices that led me to that podium on November 10, 1988. A few weeks after coming out I would support students in creating the nation's first Gay-Straight Alliance (GSA), at Concord Academy. Two years later (in 1990) I would found what became the Gay, Lesbian, and Straight Education Network (GLSEN) to provide support to those who wanted to create change in their schools. And six years later (in 1994) I would edit the first edition of *One Teacher in Ten*, hoping to provide stories that would make sure no LGBT teacher ever felt alone again.

The first edition of *One Teacher in Ten* reflected the time in which it was written. Many contributors were closeted. Some used pseudonyms for themselves, their schools, or their communities as they feared what might happen should their identities become known. The collection was a very mixed bag.

In 2004 I decided to come out with an all-new edition of the anthology, as I was curious if things had changed. Indeed they had. Virtually all contributors were "out," and success stories abounded. It was clear that progress was being made.

When I decided in 2014 to do an all-new third edition of this anthology, I was even more intrigued by what might have changed (or not changed) since I had come out more than a quarter century before. The results are in the volume you hold in your hands, which I have organized as follows:

The section "Signs of Change" features stories that reflect the progress that is being made, with stories as varied as a first-year "out" teacher in the Midwest and a veteran "out" teacher in Virginia.

"Unexpected Journeys" contains essays in which the authors describe odysseys they could not have predicted would occur, with many becoming accidental activists along the way.

"The Struggle Continues" demonstrates how much work remains to be done, even in places as seemingly accepting as Holland and New York City.

My greatest joy in editing this collection was its diversity. Contributors come from four countries (including the United States) and eleven different US states. Contributors include closeted teachers in New York City and "out" teachers in the South, defying the stereotypes that are commonly held about the levels of acceptance of LGBT people in different regions of the United States. Voices that were rare or absent from the first two editions, including those of people of color, transgender people, and people from outside the United States, now make up more than half of all contributors. The spectrum of experiences and backgrounds is inspiring.

I hope someday there will be no need for decennial editions of *One Teacher in Ten*. The inspiring stories found in this edition make me believe that day is within reach, and I profoundly thank all the contributors for sharing their stories.

—Kevin Jennings

Prologue: Forget the Rest

Mzoli

HIGH SCHOOL ENGLISH LANGUAGE
AND LITERATURE TEACHER
Cape Town, South Africa

I am _____, first.

I am not gay.

I am not brown.

I am not a woman.

Walking through the hallways, you'll see what you want to. You'll look out for my comment confirming your belief of who I am. You don't understand why I wear skirts; why I wear my hair down. You don't understand why I don't hate men. You won't try to understand. You accept that I love rugby. You accept that I love hockey. You accept that I love beer and motorbikes. You accept what you understand. But you won't accept me as I see myself.

I am _____, first.

_____ is someone who forgets her partner is a woman. She forgets her lunch at home. She forgets she's brown. She forgets to buy milk. She forgets she's gay.

I am _____ first. Forget the rest.

PART 1

Signs of Change

1

Coming Out for Owen

Alan Yount

SIXTH-GRADE TEACHER
School of the Future (M413)
New York, New York

Every year of my ten-year teaching career in New York City public schools began with the same required writing-project assignment: write a small-moment story about yourself that teaches us a life lesson or something important about you. I hated the assignment for many reasons—I was sick of reading how kids overcame fear (that they didn't have) by riding a roller coaster; how a trip to the Poconos changed their life; how beating their brother at some video game taught them about competition—but I mostly hated the assignment because of how it put me back in the closet.

I came to teaching in my forties as a New York Teaching Fellow, after careers in nursing and as a lawyer. I had been out for decades; I had been out in my previous careers; and I was out to my fellow teachers and principals and instructors. I was not, however, out to my students.

I taught fifth and sixth grades, and I never saw the need to tell them about my sexual orientation. The word *sexual* in that descriptor gave me pause in coming out to them: "Fifth or sixth graders don't need to know who I sleep with," I thought.

The buildup to that writing assignment, however, always made me think about that decision. As part of gathering ideas to write about, we would make lists—lists of important firsts (the first time I went to the playground alone, the first time I went on a plane, the

4

first time I went to a funeral); lists of important lasts (the last time I saw my grandmother, my last day at elementary school or summer camp or my home country); lists of important people (my grandmother, my father, my little sister); lists of topics that are important to the writer (bullying, littering, divorce)—and then we would look for small moments that show something important about that first or last time, that person, or that topic.

It was in those lists that I found myself back in the closet. As a teacher, I would model what I wanted the students to do. So, I would make my own lists to demonstrate what they should do in their notebooks. While I found it easy to come up with meaningful lists—the first time I ran a marathon, my first night in Guatemala as a Peace Corps Volunteer, the last time I saw my father before he died—I always left some of the most meaningful moments of my life off the lists, like the first time I met my partner. My list of important people in my life included my mother, brothers, and some close friends, but . . . it didn't include my partner. Topics that were important to me included bullying and education, but they didn't include homophobia and gay marriage, at least not on my lists. These lists represented a closeted view of me.

I told myself, "They're just sixth graders. They don't need to know about my personal life, at least not my *real* personal life." *Did I really need to tell them about me? Why would I be doing that? Was it to push my own—"the gay"—agenda? Would I be telling them in order to enrich their education or to enrich myself? What business was it of theirs anyway?* I was conflicted.

That all changed in May of 2011, my eighth year of teaching. I had two good classes that year. I really liked a lot of the kids, and I enjoyed teaching them. By May, I felt very comfortable with them.

I had a good rapport with my fellow sixth-grade teachers and the rest of the sixth-grade team, made up of our principal, the guidance counselor, and the gym teacher. All the sixth-grade core teachers ate lunch together every day, and every Thursday the entire team would come together at lunch to discuss students and what was going on in our classes. During one of those meetings, our principal informed us that she had gotten a call from the parents of Owen, one of my students.

Owen's parents had called to inform us that Owen was being picked on because, in their words, "he was perceived to be gay." They went on to say that they didn't know if he was gay or not, and they didn't care, but they wanted the bullying to stop. Owen—a very good student—no longer wanted to come to school.

We discussed the situation and how to handle it. We would talk with the students about sexuality, without identifying anyone by name. We would remind them that we had a zero-tolerance policy about bullying, and that policy applied in full force to bullying about whether someone is gay or not. We'd answer their questions and be firm but understanding. In other words, we'd do all things that a good school should be doing.

I brought up the idea of coming out to my students, which the team supported, *if* I was comfortable doing it. I went home that Thursday afternoon, struggling with the whole thing. *Should I tell them? Will it help the situation? Will my students still like me? Will I get push-back from parents? Will some parents want to move their kids out of my classroom?*

As I went back and forth, trying to decide if coming out to the students would help the situation, an incident from my own childhood came back to me. When I was in fifth grade, my teacher sent me to the guidance counselor's office. For some reason the guidance counselor, Mrs. Llewellyn, left me alone in the office while she attended to something else. I was a pretty timid kid, not prone to snooping around on an adult's desk and looking at the papers there, but . . . she was gone for a while. I began to fidget. I picked up the note on Mrs. Llewellyn's desk that was clearly from my teacher, unfolded it, and read:

"Alan is a sissy and seems to enjoy being that way."

The note went on to ask that Mrs. Llewellyn "evaluate" me. The humiliation I felt at that moment stung me, as if the words on the page penetrated my skin. I quickly refolded the note, put it back on the desk, and waited for Mrs. Llewellyn to return and do whatever was to be done to me.

The memory of that humiliation stung me again that night, and made my mind up for me. The idea of Owen being picked on— humiliated—because some kids thought he might be gay overrode my own fears and conflicts about coming out in the classroom. I called my principal to inform her that I planned on coming out to my students the following day.

Friday morning arrived after a night of tossing and turning. I actually stressed over what I should wear to school that day. I always dressed conservatively for work—khakis and a button-down, collared shirt—while my colleagues, all much younger than I, wore blue jeans and T-shirts. Should I try to look younger, more like everyone else? In the end, I wore what I always wore. After all, this was all about coming out and being myself, right?

I called the kids over to the rug (yes, sixth graders still sit on the floor on a rug) for read-aloud (yes, sixth graders still have books read aloud to them, albeit for different reasons than third graders do), and began reading and modeling my thinking about our book. I stopped suddenly, before I could change my mind, and put the book aside, "I have something that we need to talk about.

"I've seen people picking on other people in the hallways lately. They've been calling each other gay and telling them that they're disgusting. I want you to know how much that hurts me. It hurts me because . . . I'm gay.

"I'm gay, and I'm fifty years old, and it hurts my feelings when I hear someone say that. Can you imagine what it must feel like for someone your age to hear that?"

At first there was silence, but sixth graders don't stay silent about anything for long. The questions started coming in: "How did you know?" "When did you know?" "Are there other gay teachers here?" None of the questions were mean. The kids sincerely wanted to know about what being gay was like. And, some of them were concerned about me: "Do you have someone, a . . . boyfriend?"

"Yes, I have a partner, and we've been together for over twenty years."

They wanted to know more. They wanted to understand me and who I was. They cared.

Then, some of the students started talking about people in their own lives who were gay—friends of parents, friends of older siblings, relatives—and one student told the class that she has two mothers. Everyone was supportive, and all of us were closer.

As wonderful as all that was, the best was yet to come. At the end of the day, I was in the teachers' lounge, making photocopies for the next day's lesson. One of the school's secretaries escorted one of my students in to see me. The student was an African American boy—a good kid but extremely quiet and shy. He handed me a small shopping bag and said thank you to me. I opened the bag and pulled out a little plaque of Snoopy doing that ears-in-the-air Snoopy dance. Below Snoopy, the plaque read, "Be yourself! No one can ever tell you you're doing it wrong!" Tears welled up in my eyes. I held out my hand and said thank you back. He walked over to me and hugged me, and my tears came in full force. He said thank you again and walked out, leaving me in a puddle of my own tears.

Coming out to my students turned out to be one of the best things I could do. For them and for me. It created a community and opened all of us up to new ways of being together in the classroom—in the world. It opened all of us up to our shared humanity.

I told my students every year thereafter that I am gay. And, it has always been a positive experience for them and for me. It made me a better teacher—and a better person.

2

Back to School

Philip de Sa e Silva

UPPER SCHOOL ENGLISH TEACHER
St. Paul Academy and Summit School
St. Paul, Minnesota

Having just finished my first year as a high school teacher, barely a year after graduating from college, I am constantly stunned by the ways in which I feel like I am a high school student again. Something about the physical environment of a high school campus makes me revert to my teenage self in amusing ways. Occasionally, I need to be reminded that I do not have to ask for permission to go to the restroom. I once caught myself thinking absentmindedly, "Wow, I'm so excited to go to college." I sometimes enter the school cafeteria and freeze as I look out at the sea of tables as I think, *Where do I sit?* until I recall that I am an adult and that my placement in the lunchroom has little bearing on the state of the universe.

One of the most important differences, however, between my student self and my teacher self is that the last time I was in high school I was still in the closet. Now that I am back, albeit in an entirely different role, the changes I see in my own life and in the lives of the people around me make me realize how far I have come in understanding and accepting my identity and how much youth culture has changed in its acceptance of LGBTQ people.

I used to believe that one of the advantages of being a young teacher is the ability to empathize more easily with students—after all, I was a student not too long ago—and I have certainly found that my age has had many benefits in my first couple of years as a teacher.

But I have found too that, perhaps because I am gay, I have repressed a great deal of my experience in high school, probably because it was a time when I felt limited in my ability to be myself.

I grew up in a suburb of Seattle—a fairly progressive part of the country—and attended a high school I loved and for which I still feel great affection and gratitude. I knew that I had some allies among the teachers at my school (one of my favorite English teachers told us on the first day of school that he did not want to hear the word *gay* used as a negative adjective in his class because he had many friends who identified as gay). At the same time, I was very used to hearing the words *gay* and *fag* thrown around the hallways outside class—sometimes directed toward me, though I had never officially come out. One of my best friends was gay and had come out as a freshman, but I knew that his coming-out experience had been a struggle, so I determined that it would be best if I waited until college to come out, which is what I eventually did. College proved to be a hugely supportive place where I met other newly out LGBTQ people, participated in LGBTQ student life organizations, and studied queer theory, history, and issues in education. I had entered college already knowing that I wanted to be an English teacher—I love language and stories—but I discovered while in college that I also wanted to become a positive presence for LGBTQ students who may be having struggles similar to those I experienced as a high school student.

These hopes stayed with me when I began applying to teaching jobs as a senior. From my very first contact with the school where I now work, I was fortunate not to have to wonder whether I would be fully accepted as a gay person. Early in the interview process, I learned that students studied Annie Proulx's *Brokeback Mountain* in one of the English electives, that the Gay-Straight Alliance once hosted a "Queer Eye"–themed assembly in which two student-nominated faculty members received makeovers, and that the openly gay drama teacher (who sports an electric-blue pedicure every fall) was one of the most beloved members of the community. After I was hired, I learned that there are several other out faculty members in my school—some of whom have children who attend the school as well.

These discoveries have had a profoundly comforting effect on me as a new teacher—both new to the school and new to the profession. It is not lost on me that schools historically have not been welcoming to people who identify as LGBTQ. Even today—just a few minutes' drive from where I work—this continues to be so. Yet the school where I now work allows for a degree of visibility and openness that did not feel possible when I was a high school student just six years ago.

A significant part of my ability to be myself at work comes not only from the courage and openness of my colleagues but also from that of my students. One of my favorite things about my school is the senior speech program, a tradition in which every graduating senior addresses the school in a five-minute speech on a topic of the student's choice. On a gorgeous Friday morning in the fall, early on in my first year, students crowded the bleachers of the packed gymnasium to listen to a student give a speech in which she confidently and beautifully told the story of discovering and coming to terms with her identity as a lesbian. As I looked around the gym during the speech, I was struck to see that there was absolutely no disruption from any students—no whispering, no snickering, no jeering—just full, rapt attention. Toward the end of her speech, this student explained that she chose to tell her story in the hope that someone in the audience going through a similar experience would know that they are not alone and that "it gets better." The second she finished her speech, everyone in the gymnasium—students, teachers, parents, administrators—leapt to their feet to applaud this student. As I stood and clapped along with them, I felt elated and astounded that both the speech and the reaction it elicited could be possible in a school in America today. When I was in high school, I knew some openly gay students, but I could not imagine one of them discussing their identity in front of the entire school—or for the school community to affirm and embrace them so publically without hesitation.

My own official coming out to students did not take place in front of the entire school; it was totally unplanned. Since I started teaching, I had wanted to be a visible ally and potential resource, which is why I would attend GSA meetings, but I had not had an occasion to come out formally. As was the case when I was a high school student, I imagine many students had already guessed or assumed I was gay, but I had not actually said anything explicitly.

In February, my school runs a blood drive that students actively and energetically publicize at a table outside the cafeteria. During that time, I would walk briskly past the table and avoid eye contact so as not to have to explain to students why I would not be participating, even though I supported their work. But one afternoon I was in my classroom a few minutes before the start of my sophomore American literature class as students started walking in, and one of the enthusiastic blood-drive promoters asked, "Mr. de Sa e Silva, are you going to participate in the blood drive?"

"No. I can't."

"Why not?"

"Because gay men are not allowed to donate blood," I answered softly, not sure how students would react. I quickly grabbed my water bottle and took a drink to hide the fact that I was shaking slightly.

To my relief, my students were indignant. "What? That's a rule? That's crazy!" I smiled to myself at their reaction, which was much more about restrictions around blood donation than it was about me. And then we started having our discussion on *The Great Gatsby*— with no awkwardness, no disrespect.

I have found that being able to discuss all aspects of identity not only has allowed greater comfort in my school but also has enriched—and created more authentic—classroom discussions. Since joining my school community, I have been able to have conversations with students about heteronormativity, gender as a social construct, and the ways in which our language is changing to become more inclusive of people who identify as trans. I am always impressed by how openly and respectfully students—many of whom are only fifteen years old—are able to have these discussions. (For one especially memorable lesson, I asked one of my classes of sophomores if anyone had heard the word *heteronormative*, and one of my students was able to provide an eloquent and comprehensive definition for the rest of the class.) Seeing young people act with such maturity and empathy gives me hope for the state of things in the future.

So, while my old high-school self manifests itself in various ways in my new life as a teacher, there are notable ways in which it does not. I no longer shrink in my seat and stare fixedly at my desk when someone says the word *gay* in class. I do not change the pitch of my voice to a more masculine-sounding register or avoid speaking altogether. Rather than being focused on hiding things about myself to avoid harassment, my energy and attention are better spent on teaching students. And it heartens me to remember that there is at least one school in the world where students and teachers can be fully themselves—and that I have the privilege of calling this school home.

3

Teaching Trans

Ryan Ambuter

TENTH-GRADE ENGLISH LANGUAGE ARTS TEACHER
Paulo Freire Social Justice Charter School
Holyoke, Massachusetts

Like many students, I had no idea in the spring of my senior year of college what I would do after graduation. So when my mom called and said, "There's a teaching position available at a new school in New Hampshire. Maybe if you apply they'll hire you," I thought I'd give it a shot. I knew I liked working with youth and I was passionate about literacy, so I went for it and she was right.

The job was teaching seventh- through twelfth-grade English at a school for at-risk students in Milltown, a community with a 50 percent high school dropout rate. I was attracted to the students this school would serve: the ones who had already dropped out of the public high school, who were expected to go nowhere, who had a history of trauma and conflict. From coursework and personal experience, I understood that it can be impossibly hard to thrive in poor, rural communities and that these are places where capable, compassionate teachers are most needed. I also understood that rural communities without much exposure to diversity can be difficult or unsafe for LGBTQ people. I was afraid I was walking into one of those cases, but I decided to take the job anyway. That is how in May of 2004, after spending four years immersed in trans and queer activism at Smith College, I found myself moving from Northampton, Massachusetts, to middle-of-nowhere New Hampshire.

I was drawn to Milltown, but I didn't feel particularly comfortable there. It seemed to be a very conservative, insular community, so I chose to live about twenty-five minutes away in a bigger town with a Borders bookstore and a slight liberal presence. I figured I was unlikely to see students there and would be able to be myself in the evenings and on the weekends. I was young and green and an employee at will in a workplace without an inclusive nondiscrimination code. I had yet to develop the self-assurance about being out in the classroom that I feel today. Then, I was just trying to stay safe and make it as a first-year teacher without getting fired, so I started to grow my hair out, decided to leave my men's clothes at home, and kept my mouth shut.

In Milltown I became "Ms. Ambuter," Ms. Ambuter who wore fitted shirts and women's pants and shoes with a little heel. I feel uncomfortable now just writing about it. I'd go to school and be that person, and then I'd come home and immediately take off my women's clothes, pull on jeans, a button-down, a tie, a leather jacket. I'd spike my hair, and when I recognized the person in the mirror as me, I'd hop in the car. Most days I'd drive to Borders, find a book, and sit for hours. I had moved to Milltown alone and didn't know other queer or trans folks, but it didn't matter. I needed to be visible, at least to myself.

Even with the dissonance of being Ms. Ambuter at work, I really liked my job. The only hard part was the daily, extended visits by John Grinch, an aptly named school-board member. He wielded a lot of power over town and school politics, was deeply homophobic, and had a large, intimidating presence. To him, there was absolutely a right way and a wrong way to live. We knew it, his wife knew it, his son Graham, who was in my eighth-grade class, knew it too.

Graham was a sweet, soft-spoken kid who slouched and looked at the ground when he talked. "Ms. Ambuter?" he'd say.

"Yes, Graham?"

"Where does Santa put the Jewish people's presents?"

"He doesn't. Jewish people don't celebrate Christmas."

"Really?" Graham was sheltered. Many of my students were. There were so many ideas and lifestyles they had been given little opportunity to learn about.

Later that day, he tentatively asked, "Um, Ms. Ambuter?"

"Yes?"

"You know those people who are boys but they want to be girls?" Oh boy, did I.

"Transgender people, Graham. That's the word."

"Oh."

"Mm-hmm?"

"Well, do they have their own holidays?" He did not mean Pride.

"Transgender people can celebrate any holiday, Graham. Just like you and me."

"Oh. Thank you." And here my stories of being trans and being a teacher began to overlap.

Graham was undeniably curious, and undeniably gay. I don't know his internal process, but he found a book on my shelf, *The Geography Club*, about a gay boy in high school, and read it half a dozen times before asking, "Ms. Ambuter? Can you buy me a copy of that book if I give you money?" So I stopped by Borders on my way home and brought it to him the next day.

Later that week his mom came to my classroom. She was a thin, pale woman with light, light eyes, alcohol on her breath, and a nervous disposition. "Thank you for supporting Graham, but I think he needs books with a little more . . . diversity. You know, sports, basketball, that kind of thing. I'm not against him reading books like that. I just want him to read books with more *diversity*," she emphasized.

"Okay. I understand." I did. I understood that there would be no more gay books for her son. In that moment I also understood that she wasn't the one with the problem. She was trying to protect her son from his father, and her conversation with me had an undertone of sadness and resignation. There wasn't much more to say.

The next time he asked me to go to Borders, this time for *Queer as Folk*, I said, "Graham, I can't get you anything with gay characters. Your mom asked me not to."

"Oh. Okay." He didn't give much of a reaction.

"I'm so sorry. But you do have a library card. I'm sure if there's something you want, you can find a way to get it." He gave me half a smile and the year moved on. I didn't know how to support him, so I bought more LGBTQ books, put them on my classroom bookshelves, and hoped Graham would find them on his own. I was afraid to talk to him directly about it—afraid for him and for my job—and I let my fears stop me.

That spring I resigned from the Milltown school and applied to a social justice graduate program, writing my admissions essays about my first teaching experience: About being told not to read *To Kill a Mockingbird* because it was too controversial. About the time the whole school was called together and told we needed to publicly support George W. Bush. About kids like Graham, who were silenced, sheltered, and in need of support. About my own lack of visibility. About how much Graham might have benefited from seeing a queer adult who was successful and happy. Not just Graham but any kid there—the ones who were progressive, the ones who were staunchly conservative, the ones who just weren't exposed to much besides their little town. Everyone benefits from knowing that other options exist. I've always been drawn to stories of LGBTQ elders who were visible and proud in the face of serious adversity. Some lost their loves, their communities, their careers, their lives. And they gave us ours by creating the visibility necessary to inspire a social movement for authenticity and pride. I could have joined in, been one of the people I so admire. I could have lived that year in a way I was proud of. But I didn't, and I regret it. When I left Milltown, I vowed never to compromise myself like that again.

The summer after I graduated with my master's degree and teacher certification, I got a phone call. The warm voice introduced himself as Richard Wilde, a newly hired principal whose ninth-and-tenth-grade English teacher had just quit. It was late July. He explained that he had my résumé on file from when I'd applied to his previous school years ago. "Do you have a job?"

"Well, no. I have an offer, but I haven't signed a contract."

One week and one interview later I signed on to teach ninth- and tenth-grade English at a small, progressive school in western Massachusetts. I still remember what I wore on my first day of work: a maroon button-down shirt with the sleeves rolled up, tucked into brown cargo pants. Getting dressed and going to work feeling like myself was exciting, and that feeling carried me through my first few years.

In my third year, I noticed a student in my tenth-grade classroom, Harper, who was new to the school. Most students enter this school in seventh grade, so students who enter in the upper grades are noticeable. Right away her short-haired, baggy-clothed, layered appearance caught my attention—something about it was familiar to me. Coincidentally, a student in the same class who had done a project on transgender people the year before came by one day to return a few of my books she had borrowed for her research: *Transgender Warriors* and *Trans Liberation: Beyond Pink and Blue*. I was holding them as I walked around the classroom, and without thinking about it too much I set them on the table in front of Harper. "Here. You might like these. They're mine. You can keep them as long as you want." I hung around her table for a minute, waiting for a response. She looked at the titles, smiled to herself, and put the books in her messenger bag and slid it back under the table. I didn't want to make her uncomfortable, but I wanted to say something more. "You know, gender is something I spend a lot of time thinking about, if you ever want to talk." She ducked her head and nodded, and I walked away.

She was great in my class, but we didn't really connect until a few weeks later during one of my prep periods, when she brought the books up to my desk. Harper lingered there for a minute, looking down at the books and then back at me.

"What'd you think?" I asked.

"I liked them . . ." She trailed off and then started again. "I started reading stuff about gender in middle school." Reaching into her bag, she pulled out a folded set of papers and handed them to me. It was an essay about transvestites and trans-fetishism—outdated language that neither of us would use today—that she had written in seventh grade. Her teacher's comment across the top read: "Wow, Harper! This is intense!"

Harper mentioned to me that she was questioning her gender. She didn't seem ready to talk about much but clearly was looking for connection. She showed up in my room two or three times a week. We'd work on an art project and make small talk, or she'd do her work and I'd do mine. I'm not sure how our conversations shifted into something more personal, but by winter we were talking about gender and identity and transition.

I'd learned as a young camp counselor that there are complicated, unclear lines when it comes to adult-youth relationships. People outside the relationship tend to sexualize perfectly appropriate mentor-mentee bonding between LGBTQ adults and LGBTQ youth, so I was careful to set very strong boundaries. I knew some people would see our connection and have a problem with it simply because we were both visibly queer. When Harper and I were alone in my classroom, I made sure my door was wide open and I sat behind my desk. Harper, who by this point was using "he, him, his" pronouns, would sit on the table nearest to my desk. One day as he was building a little tower out of my office supplies, I asked him how gender things were going.

"I want top surgery," he replied.

"Yeah?" I said. I paused, then added, "I'm having mine this summer."

He seemed really excited and had a lot of questions. While I felt vulnerable answering them, I remembered Graham and how disappointed I was with myself for not being forthright about my queerness. I thought about how much I would have benefited from an out teacher, how much I benefit from other people's outness and willingness to share. I also thought about why I teach. To me teaching is not just about course content and skill building; it's also about empowering youth to live meaningfully and authentically. I wasn't naive to the consequences of someone misinterpreting my relationship with Harper, but I decided that being a mentor to him was right and worth the risk. I answered as many of his questions as I could, gave him resources, and recommended a local trans youth support group.

Around this time, I came out as trans at work. It felt necessary and important for myself, for Harper, and for the other students at the school. I wanted to be proud of my actions, so I stopped sidestepping gender. I had direct conversations of my own, telling my boss that I was having chest surgery that summer and also that I couldn't come back to work as Ms. anything. I asked again if teachers could use first names as an alternative to Mr. or Ms. "Well," he said, "there are a lot of ways that we are informal, and last names feel important to me. I haven't felt flexible about that because no one has had a compelling reason for the policy to change. But you have a compelling reason. Do you want to be 'Mr. Ambuter'?"

I didn't.

"Can you think of alternatives to your first name?"

I suggested simply going by "Ambuter" to students. He was fine with that, and I wondered why I hadn't thought of it sooner. It was an easy shift for students, and one that felt honest to me.

The next fall, it felt equally authentic but much scarier when I wrote "trans/queer" on my nametag before our school's Coming Out Day assembly. After I affixed the sticker to my chest, I saw Harper glance at it and do the same to his nametag. Even though I wasn't his teacher anymore, Harper still managed to find his way to my classroom most days. He had become an active trans leader in our school community with a solid sense of self and had scheduled his top surgery for November 17, one month after his eighteenth birthday.

I remember the day he came into my classroom and said, "Ambuter, my mom is taking me to top surgery in Boston and she doesn't want to do it alone."

"Can your dad go?"

"My dad offered to take work off, but he's being weird about it, and I don't want him there." Harper continued, "My mom and I were talking about who could come that we would both be comfortable with, and she suggested you."

And so I went. After we saw Harper off to surgery, his mom and I went for a walk and found a coffee shop. "Can I treat you?" she asked. I ordered a small hot chocolate, and we sat down at a little round table. We hadn't ever talked much, and I felt slightly awkward as we looked out the window and sipped our drinks in silence.

"Ambuter?" She was so used to hearing her kid refer to me that way that she did too. "Thank you for being there for Harper."

I had come a long way.

A lot has changed since my first year teaching: my nonnegotiables, my body, my name, my confidence and comfort in the classroom. As a college student, I identified strongly as an activist. I used to believe that my activism stopped when I started teaching. These days, I consider teaching with authenticity my activism.

I am in my sixth year as an out trans teacher, and I've had a handful of students come out to me as trans since then. Many use my class as a place to explore LGBTQ topics, and more ask me honest questions and receive honest answers. I don't dodge the topics my students want to engage in, and I am less afraid when others find fault in my candor, because I believe in myself as a teacher. There is something about seeing yourself in someone, about exposure and options, that helps people come into their own. I am not making my students trans or queer, but I am living my life. When that helps LGBTQ youth feel empowered to live theirs, I'm glad.

Coming into a solid sense of self and navigating that identity through time and place isn't easy. Over the past ten years there have been many times that I've thought about how much simpler it would be, professionally, if I were a different type of trans. I could grow a beard, go by "Mr.," and "fully transition" into a more binary identity, but that has never been who I am. In the end, I like my short hair, flat chest, smooth face, higher voice, male-sounding name, no-fitting-pronoun-or-title self. A series of contradictions make me visible in the classroom every day, and that visibility matters. Through my teaching, my activism, I try to show that there are many ways to do gender, many ways to identify as anything, and no one is more legitimate or worthy than another. I choose to be authentic and unapologetic in the classroom, and I hope that makes it a little easier for my students to be themselves too.

4

Everyone Knows Now

Carmen Neely

SPECIAL EDUCATION TEACHER
UFT Elementary Charter School MS-326—Brooklyn, NY
New York, New York

I was in my seventh year of teaching during the 2010–11 school year. Having taught middle-school special education for my entire career, this year was particularly challenging as I was teaching first grade for the first time, and I was concerned about how parents of young children may feel about their child having a lesbian teacher. I was not closeted, but I also didn't walk around with an L on my forehead.

It also happens that, through a series of fortunate events, I was president and cofounder of Harlem Pride, Inc., Harlem, New York's Same-Gender-Loving/LGBT advocacy group. Our main event was an annual Pride celebration in June, and at the time we were planning our second-annual Harlem Pride Celebration. Generally speaking, it had been easy to keep my school activities separate from my Harlem Pride activities. The two never really intersected. However, one evening in June about two weeks before our celebration date, I was asked to do an interview for the second-largest newspaper in the city. I'd never done a newspaper interview and was excited to do it. During the interview, the reporter informed me that some local ministers were protesting our annual Pride celebration, which was to be held in a park near their churches, and asked for my thoughts about their objections. I responded that our time as a Same-Gender-Loving/ LGBT community had come, and that we weren't going to let a group of ministers stop us from exercising our right to celebrate. Giving the interview felt wonderful. I called my board members and told them the interview had gone well. We were already quite well known in Harlem and hoped this article would help introduce us to the rest of the city and get more people out to our second-annual Pride celebration.

Well, little did I know that the article (which was published the very next day) would start a media frenzy. I was at school when I first saw it, picture and all, shown to me by a colleague who was supportive but concerned. I panicked. I was afraid that parents would see the article and request a new teacher for their child, or that my principal might all of a sudden think I wasn't such a great teacher after all and give me a poor evaluation. All at once, my school life and personal life collided, and I was totally blindsided. I was nervous and afraid and found it hard to concentrate at work. However, I was determined to stand tall, walk with my head up, and deal with things as best as I could.

The media frenzy led to a morning television news interview that I was terrified to do, but I knew I could not back down. The next day, after the interview, when I entered the teachers' lounge, several colleagues gave me silent nods of solidarity; others were guarded and distant. It was difficult not knowing exactly who was and who was not an ally. I was extremely uncomfortable and had never felt so scrutinized. Sitting down to do my work, I tried to act as normal as possible. The next few days were difficult as I continued to feel nervous and emotionally fragile. Though I did worry about what my colleagues thought and felt about me, I kept telling myself that it just didn't matter. The paranoia, hypersensitivity, and resulting energy put toward trying to act "normal" were draining. I would go home and pass out immediately.

Over time, things did get back to normal. I calmed down and colleagues generally seemed more relaxed in my company. Only a few remained distant. Luckily, those few weren't people with whom I had to work closely. At least I didn't have to wonder who knew I was a lesbian, because they all knew now. Whatever they thought, or didn't think, about that was beyond my control. As I slowly embraced that fact and let go of my fears, a weight that I hadn't even realized I'd been carrying was lifted. I was living more authentically than I ever had. It felt delicious! I was freer than ever. Going to work was no longer as stressful as it had been. My interactions with my colleagues were more congenial. I had a newfound sense of purpose, pride, and confidence. In fact, this newfound authenticity, coupled with a fierce, unapologetic honesty, became the silver lining to my media frenzy thundercloud.

In the end, not one parent requested a change of teachers, and I succeeded in earning yet another year-end satisfactory evaluation. I felt accepted and no longer feared being discriminated against or ostracized.

Despite the ministers' protest, our second-annual Pride celebration was a grand success, having thousands more participants than the previous year. In fact, several prominent ministers from historic Harlem churches wrote letters of support, and we received proclamations from three of our local politicians. Thanks to the controversy, Harlem Pride got much more news coverage than in the previous year, and we were certainly one of the media darlings of New York City's Pride month. What I thought would be a nightmare ended up helping me grow tremendously as a person. Previously I felt that I was as out of the closet as I could be. Now I was not only out of the closet, but I was also able to turn around and close that closet door.

Not that all has been smooth sailing ever since. Being a middle-school special education teacher can be frustrating, particularly when dealing with students whose brains and hormones can lead to difficult behavior. Add to that the quandary of being a lesbian teacher while watching young Same-Gender-Loving/LGBT students go through their changes, feeling bound by a system that dares you to risk your career by exposing yourself as a would-be mentor or confidant. It's painful standing on the sidelines when I see Same-Gender-Loving/LGBT youth in my school working through their issues. I wish I were at liberty to say, "Hi, I've been there and I'm here if you want to talk." However, these very words, if misconstrued, can mean the end of your teaching career. There have been many teachers whose careers were cut short by accusations of inappropriate behavior with a student.

Despite these inherent frustrations, I have made it my business to be as crafty as possible on behalf of our budding Same-Gender-Loving/ LGBT leaders, vigilantly watching for any opportunity to support a Same-Gender-Loving/LGBT youth. One fine day while descending the stairs from my fourth floor classroom, I happened upon "Miles" standing jubilantly on the landing below while a female student applied mascara and eye shadow to his usually well-made-up face. I had suspected he might be one of "ours" and I stopped on the stairs to appreciate the openness of the students in our school. We have very few incidents of bullying.

However, Miles must have felt the weight of my stare, because upon making eye contact with me, he pushed his young makeup artist away and began acting as if she were forcing him to allow her to apply the makeup. He even went so far as to call for my assistance in escaping his would-be assailant. She, looking at me bewildered, professed her innocence. I, however, gave Miles a "now, you know better" look and continued to walk down the stairs. I felt uneasy and did not like his negative reaction upon realizing I was watching. I was disappointed that he felt embarrassed and wished I had not stopped to watch.

I didn't see Miles again until the next day when he ran me down in the hallway to explain that he was being forced to have mascara put on his lashes. He wanted to assure me that he would never actually want—much less enjoy—such a thing. Amused, I waited calmly for him to finish and said, "My dear Miles, never apologize for being who and what you are, and most certainly don't lie about it. You are a beautiful person just as you are. As a matter of fact, I thought the black mascara looked good on you. Next time, you might try midnight blue. It'd go lovely with your eye color." His jaw dropped. He was utterly speechless. I smiled and walked away.

Rules and regulations be damned: I will find a way to affirm and acknowledge our Same-Gender-Loving/LGBT youth whenever and however possible.

5

Just the Normal Stuff

Deidre Cuffee-Gray

COUNSELOR
Springfield Renaissance School
Springfield, Massachusetts

Twenty minutes late to a meeting at the start of the school year and suddenly nothing is new. I'm notorious for my tardiness both at work and in life. My pledge of timeliness has disintegrated on the fifth day of school.

A family meeting in the first week of school is certainly not a good sign. This, for a student whom we all consider extremely bright and extremely troubled, whose combative and provocative actions had us resolved to call her parents on the first day. We approached this call with trepidation as we knew the parents could be pretty irascible and neither hesitated to speak their minds. Last year the student was the seventh grade's "Don Juanita," slaying a cohort of girls who "date girls but aren't lesbians," and this year she is sagging her pants deeper than anyone in the school, grades six through twelve.

I hustle down the hallway and find Mr. and Mrs. exiting the main office, and I resolve to engage them in conversation. After our customary greetings, despite my better angels, I offer to accompany them outside so we can chat. Even though I'm freaking late, I have to do the work that I'm paid for.

"They said she's sagging her pants," Dad says.

"Yes. She doesn't leave the house that way?" I innocently ask.

"What? No, no, no. Her pants are up to her rib cage when she leaves," says the mother.

Dad assures me that this will end.

Gulp.

"What she think? She a *dude*? *She gay*?" He's raising his voice now, "No, no, no. She is going to hear from *me* tonight."

Before I can think straight I strongly (and, strangely, calmly) say, "The issue isn't if she's gay. If she's gay, that's fine. She's just not meeting the dress code."

The two are atypically quiet and considering the craziness I just spoke.

"Look, it is not about how she sees herself. She can be gay. She just needs to figure out that it is okay to be her smart self. We know she's super smart. And I'm worried that she's missing a chance to meet her potential," I quietly assert. I'm feeling the hand of Buddha. Centered, calm. Strangely, I'm not completely freaked out.

We end agreeing that we are going to work together to try and get this girl to stop fighting and accept that she is smart and can do school. We are on the precipice of a three-day weekend, and I will worry how it will all go down for this student for the next seventy-two hours.

As the two thank me, wave, and drive off, I take quiet inventory of how calm I feel after this crazy conversation. I feel like I know what I am doing, and I am doing it right where I need to be doing it.

It had been more than a decade since I had left a lifetime of attending and teaching in progressive independent schools where things were pretty darn peachy keen. You may know the scene—Gay-Straight Alliances, home tailored "Love Makes a Family" exhibits, Pride marches. I was terrified of working in public schools. Discussions like the one I just described were what I'd been terrified of. After all, weren't communities of color more homophobic and less accepting of their LGBTQ kids? Wouldn't I be rejected by my students and their families when I came out? Everything I'd heard about urban public schools and homophobia was negative, and I was petrified of making the move to public schools.

Okay. I went ahead and raised my hand this year. The Gay-Straight Alliance at the Springfield Renaissance School needed an advisor; both faculty advisors had left the school and the group needed someone to step in. So, I raised my hand. Into the fray, I guess.

It was not lost on me that GLSEN and GSAs have been following me around my entire adult life. I joined the Gay and Lesbian Teachers Network sometime in 1996 as the organization's third employee. I hopped out of the relative comfort of a lifetime in independent schools to become the office manager of this tiny not-for-profit focused on making schools safer. My colleagues Kevin Jennings and John Spear cleared out a space and added a desk for me. We were doing something earth shattering and revolutionary, and the office was filled with the sound of modems connecting to the Internet, strewn with fund-raising envelopes and empty take-out cartons from the awesome Indian restaurant a couple of blocks away. I met a bunch of courageous educators and activists and, at the time, it was rare that we interacted with students. Mostly, we worked with educators from around the nation trying to design protections against losing their jobs because of their sexual orientation. More and more Gay-Straight Alliances were popping up, in schools. Students were standing up. But at first, it was a strictly adult conversation.

Students changed that. If being an LGBT educator was difficult, being a student in a hostile school environment was triply difficult. There were school buses, empty bathrooms, hallways, and the deaf ears of adults to contend with every day in school. I met some courageous young people who pushed us adults to be more inclusive and more activist, which makes sense: young people are what so many movements depend upon to question the status quo. And yet, even with the infusion of the students' energy, the conversation remained fairly white. I didn't meet many educators of color at GLSEN, and never any students. The word on the street was it was harder to be African American and queer, or Latino and queer, or Asian American and queer—culture, socioeconomics, and religion made it harder for people of color to come out. I was stunned that when facilitating an adult group, the Audre Lorde Project in Fort Greene, Brooklyn, the most contentious conversation erupted around being out at work. The group included many teachers, and none were out in their schools. How could it be that these very queer people, who were out in every other aspect of their lives, couldn't be out in their schools? In New York City? Lots of them told me that when they joined existing activists' groups, the conversation would inevitably degenerate to the unaddressed biases that white organizers held on to, and people of color would leave.

I have to admit, my coming-out story is pretty tame. My family and extended family accept me for who I am, and I have lived among privileged white progressives. I have had a privileged existence as a student of color and an educator of color in independent schools. I have always had the language and the tools for challenging the insidious racism and bias that exist in my worlds. I can handle those slings and arrows pretty comfortably.

I simply accepted the assumption that it was harder to come out in communities of color, and I didn't interrogate that thinking for a while.

While I left GLSEN to return to independent schools and, eventually, become licensed as a school counselor, I was lucky enough to remain connected as a counselor with the organizing work GLSEN was doing among students of color. Nearly fifteen years after I joined GLSEN, queer kids of color were filling a hotel floor and learning organizing skills to make their schools and communities more accepting. They schooled me on the complexities of their identities and their resilience. These young people came from urban, suburban, and rural communities, and their fire to create change floored me. The face of the work had changed drastically since I was hanging out licking envelopes in that cramped GLSEN office.

It is crazy what has changed in a relatively short period of time. I was a long way from the lily-white peachy keenness of the independent school world I had inhabited for so many years.

Short story long, I ended up working at an urban public school in Springfield, Massachusetts. My school is primarily made up of students of color—46 percent Latino and 35 percent African American.

While the school's focus on climate and culture made for a relatively safe place when I started, it still wasn't unusual to overhear high school students (mostly boys) refer to someone as a faggot or something as gay. Depending on who was present, hallways and unmonitored classrooms might be peppered with the language. I once walked into a classroom where two sophomore boys were simulating "prison sex" on each other in an attempt to prove who was top dog and get laughs from classmates. These were two big guys who carried more than their share of bravado. I was completely terrified when I interrupted them, but I knew I'd be supported by my principal and I called them on their behavior. Their initial indignation about the instance "not meaning anything" was quickly addressed by a full-court press of education and consequences from administrators and advisors. When it was over, they knew they were expected to play an active role maintaining a safe space at our school.

What I have had to confront is my assumption that it is harder to be out in communities of color. If I had held on to my notion that communities of color tend to be less accepting, I wouldn't have come out. Today, my wife's picture is on my desk. I wouldn't have been available to my students who are questioning their identities or working to confront the homophobia of their peers or their families. When I arrived at the Springfield Renaissance School I found a group of colleagues committed to creating a culture of safety and acceptance. Teachers are out. No Name Calling Week and Day of Silence (a national event where students are silent for one day to symbolize the *daily* silencing of LGBT students) come and go without incident. When I go to my town's big Gay Pride March, in Northampton, I just accept the fact that I'll see half my students skipping around, marching, and celebrating. I don't hide from the students; the students don't hide from me. It isn't a big deal, and the Pride March is not the first time that they've met my partner. All that most students do is skip over to say hello, and then they're off to their adolescent lives.

This year we had no fewer than five seniors who were out at school. Many of them have been out since middle school. A couple of students transferred into Renaissance as sophomores and juniors knowing that ours was a school environment that would be accepting of who they were. While coming out was not easy for any of them, the fact that they were in a supportive environment and had allies—teachers, advisors, faculty, and peers—helps create a culture of safety and belonging. It's okay to be smart and it's okay to be queer, things that may not be givens at other schools. Each of their mothers was at graduation celebrating their accomplishments and crying about their babies growing up and leaving for college. Just the normal stuff.

What creating a safe and inclusive school does is allow young LGBT people to *be adolescents when they are adolescents*. So, the conversations that I have with them are about breakups, missed homework assignments, social media disasters, and college planning. Just the normal stuff.

These are urban kids, kids of color, in a place where I'd assumed it was so much harder to be out. An Expeditionary Learning school, Renaissance is part of a network of schools that has an explicit pledge to create a climate where students can thrive both academically and emotionally. More important, there are structures that impel a culture of acceptance and inclusion. Students are required to enact that awareness in their day-to-day lives, and this has dynamically changed the place in a few short years. And yes, there is still homophobia among students, and adults say unenlightened things as well, but there is a foundation for dealing with it that provides us with the courage to interrupt that language and thinking when it occurs. Slowly, inclusion is becoming just the normal stuff.

6

Yankee in the Southland

Patty Smith

LITERARY ARTS AND ENGLISH TEACHER
Appomattox Regional Governor's School
Petersburg, Virginia

When I start teaching writing and American literature at the Appomattox Regional Governor's School for the Arts and Technology (ARGS) in Petersburg, Virginia, I'm nearing fifty with twenty-one years of teaching experience behind me. This is my first foray into public school teaching, my first time at the high school level. I'm worried what it will be like to be a gay teacher in the South, if it's okay to be a gay teacher. I'm relieved to learn that the school has already established a Gay-Straight Alliance and excited that they're looking for a new faculty sponsor. But I'm nervous about a lot of things, too: if I'll be able to follow the rules and survive, if I can withstand the deadening public-school minutiae, if I'm going to be able to be myself in this setting. Before coming to ARGS, I taught French in a private middle school in Cambridge, Massachusetts, in a combined fifth- and sixth-grade classroom, and then several years at Virginia Commonwealth University, first as an adjunct and then a full-time faculty member, where I also received my MFA in writing. While at VCU, I volunteered to help with the admissions work for ARGS. Although a public high school, eighth graders have to audition for a spot. I helped with the literary arts adjudication, and after my first experience with both the hopeful middle-school writers and the current

ARGS students, I was smitten. "It's the high school I always wished I had gone to," I told the literary arts chairperson. "Call me if you ever have an opening."

It is immediately clear to my ARGS students that I'm not "from here." When they learn I'm from Massachusetts, they nod knowingly; it all makes sense—my no-nonsense approach, my speech patterns, my bluntness, all characteristics, my students tell me, of Northerners.

I'm a Northerner living in the South, a liberal in a conservative state, a lesbian in the Bible Belt.

And a teacher.

Luckily, because it's a high school for the arts, being openly gay isn't terribly difficult. The GSA—recently renamed Spectrum at the students' request, to be more inclusive of the trans kids who feel the name Gay-Straight Alliance doesn't speak to their needs—grows to be one of the largest clubs in the school with approximately fifty kids who attend regularly. In my third year at ARGS, I meet my partner; she is a new hire, the head of the theater department and the technical theater director for the school. The kids label us a couple before we ever acknowledge it ourselves, and when we chaperone prom together that first year, the kids grin at us knowingly.

"Y'all are so cute," they say. We blush and grin back. We're a little giddy ourselves, dressed up in fancy outfits, black pants and dressy tops. We go to dinner beforehand, and I feel like one of the kids. I never attended prom as a student, a fact that made me feel like something was wrong with me, that I must be hideous or boring or both. But in my Massachusetts high school, you couldn't attend prom on your own or with friends; you had to have a date. My partner and I are not the first same-sex couple to attend ARGS prom together. Gay kids go with straight kids, girls with girls, boys with boys. Kids attend in groups or show up on their own. At my first ARGS prom, a boy was crowned queen and a girl crowned king.

Still, there are challenges. Our previous executive director (aka the principal), while supportive of the GSA's right to exist and our right to celebrate the Day of Silence, still felt the need to meet with me every year just to be sure we weren't "promoting" homosexuality, a fireable offense, he tells me, for a teacher in Virginia.

What exactly does that mean? I ask him. "Are we saying, 'Come be gay with us'? No, of course not. Are we saying, 'It's fine to be gay'? Yes, we are. If that's 'promoting' homosexuality, then maybe we are." He didn't like that answer much. When students participate in the Day of Silence, inevitably there are a few whose parents keep them home that day. There have been students themselves who have protested against the Day of Silence, too, wearing Bible verses pinned to their clothing, proclaiming with handout cards that this is a day of "loudness" and taunting the kids who maintain vows of silence. There are parents who have harassed the executive director for allowing the day to take place at all, but he steadfastly supports its right and ours to exist. I am uplifted when I come to school for the most recent Day of Silence and the line of kids wearing red T-shirts and waiting to get "talking cards" and DOS stickers wends its way from my classroom door and down the hallway. I run out of everything before the last kid makes it to my room.

For the past couple of years, though, word on the street is that ARGS is easiest if you're a gay kid, that it's tough to be conservative and Christian. I have to laugh. That's not my experience, though I do find it a refreshingly open environment. I'm not sure it's ever easier to be gay and especially not in the South with its emphasis on church and family. Secretly, part of me is thrilled to hear this new perception of ARGS, but I also know it speaks to a tension between the conservative Christian kids—both white kids and kids of color—and those kids who tend to be more open about having LGBT teachers and classmates. While many of them are genuine in their beliefs, the conservative Christian kids are firm about the Bible and its stance against homosexuality: you can't be gay and "saved." And there are those kids—their friends—who defend others' rights to believe what they believe. "You can't fault them," one kid tells me, "if that's what they believe." But after one such discussion, I have a moment I'm not proud of, and I raise my voice and tell the small class of fiction writers in front of me that I'm "so tired of people using religion as a way to hide and justify their bigotry." I know I offend a couple of kids, one girl in particular, and later I apologize. But truthfully, it is how I feel and I *am* tired of it.

The tension isn't a new one, and a few years ago, the GSA kids and I decided to hold a conversation with Youth Alive, the Christian student group (renamed more recently the Association of Christian Athletes).

We gathered in the gym during our club meeting time and participated in a fish bowl exercise, first with the GSA leaders sitting in the middle, surrounded by a mixture of GSA and Youth Alive members. We were a pretty large group and our circle covered a wide area of the gym floor. There was lots of excited chatter before we started, lots of nervous energy. We instructed kids not to sit next to their friends, and they were squeezed into the circle, smiling at the kids next to them. "Can I sit here?" "Hey, how are you?" They were trying to be light, but I recall thinking they were feeling as I did—stomach clenched, sweating, hoping that things wouldn't get out of hand, that we all could really listen and respond without anger. When I looked around, I saw a mix of faces, white, black, brown.

Both clubs had solicited questions from each other about our prejudices and biases, about things we genuinely wanted to know: Does being Christian mean you can't support LGBT equality? I've heard that being gay is a choice, so why do you choose to be gay? My church says being gay is wrong but I think gay people shouldn't be discriminated against. What should I do? Don't you think Jesus would have supported LGBT people? Do all Christians hate gay people?

My GSA kids in the middle circle talked. They offered their opinions and answered the questions, and the outside circle listened. The gym was quiet, only some shifting on the floor, an occasional cough. But kids' attention seemed focused, eyes on the center. No one whispered. No one poked the kid next to him. No one guffawed or laughed, no one shouted out. The listening was deep.

When time was up, the inner circle switched to leaders of Youth Alive. Discussion resumed. Same quiet, same focused attention. I walked around the outer circle, listening too, watching the kids. In the outer circle, some heads nodded, some faces frowned. One or two kids glanced up and shared a look with me. *Hey*, they all seemed to be saying, *this is going okay.*

Our club meeting time is only forty-five minutes, so clearly no major differences were resolved that day, but we had started a conversation. When the bell rang and the meeting block was over, the kids applauded. Any tension or nervousness was released, and the kids erupted into chatter, upbeat. "Hey bro, I feel ya," hands clasped, a pat on the back. We had seen each other as people and not as labels, and that was a start. We had even dispelled some myths or at least poked holes in one or two, so maybe now fewer kids will point fingers at each other. And each club might have even gained a few new supporters. We know this is something we should continue each year, though because of time constraints, we have yet to repeat it. Maybe now, more than ever, this conversation is needed again, with same-sex marriage now legal in Virginia, with the conservative kids feeling marginalized at our school.

Even as our little school gets a reputation among some students that it's a great place to be gay, we don't want to get complacent. We can't. Each year new students come from middle schools without GSAs, schools—and families—where it still is not cool to be gay. And now, we have a few brave trans students who are paving the way for all the others who will inevitably follow.

I'm pleased to see how much the kids in the GSA—in Spectrum—already know about gender identity. During one meeting when we do "Step to the Line," and I read the statement "Step to the line if you don't identify as either male or female" and one student does, I'm hopeful. Change, I am reminded again, often starts with the young.

Back in my early days of teaching in Massachusetts, back before GLSEN and then even in its infancy, I remember a lot of fear, the paper bags we wore at Gay Pride, the word *teacher* written to let people know. We teachers were nervous about coming out but certain, too, that doing so would have a positive impact on our students. We—some of us, that is—treaded lightly, gingerly taking steps forward to be our whole selves in the classroom. But these days, as I enter my thirtieth year of teaching, the struggles are less about me and my sexual orientation, about how that affects me as a teacher, and more about how I can support the students and the struggles they face.

We have to help administrators figure out how to implement gender-neutral bathrooms, help the coach when the transgendered young man who plays soccer wonders where to change uniforms at away games, and help remind everyone about using preferred pronouns, that we all have the right to self-define, that gender isn't a fixed binary. We like to think of ourselves as an accepting school—I like to think of our school that way—but there is still a lot of work to do.

Even in the rather open environment of ARGS, one trans student attempts suicide. Other trans students tell me about kids who constantly misgender them, use the wrong name when referring to them. Teachers do it too, they tell me. It's unnerving and I can't get what is so hard about calling someone the name they want to be called, using the pronoun they prefer using. I can't even imagine what it's like in other schools, where my students might get beaten or even killed, because if they struggle in our school, how in God's name do they thrive elsewhere? In my thirtieth year of teaching, the struggles can feel sadly endless and sometimes overwhelming.

As a writing teacher, among other things I teach kids to think about their persona on the page. Who are they when they write? How do they want to come across to the reader? In both writing and literature classes, we talk about all their various selves, the ones that, in order to do their best learning, have to merge in the classroom but sometimes don't—the selves they temporarily leave behind in their neighborhoods or sometimes abandon outright like their old friends at their home schools. We talk about identity and language and how it all ties together—the language they use to address their friends, their parents and teachers, how sometimes the African American kids are accused of "talking white" when they are back with neighborhood friends, how the language they all use for their response journals is markedly different and often much livelier than the language they use for paper writing, how this merging of their various selves is sometimes tricky.

We talk, too, about voice in writing, how it is so important but ever elusive, and especially, I add, when that voice isn't connected to the self, when the voice feels arbitrary or forced. How else to convince the reader that a real person is behind the words on the page than to put a real person behind the words on the page—flaws and all? That elusive search for identity drives most of our literary discussions as well—about Hester Prynne, about Bartleby and Huck Finn, about Gatsby, Emerson, and Thoreau. Walt Whitman and *Song of Myself*. Toni Morrison and *The Bluest Eye*. About Frederick Douglass and Harriet Jacobs. *How the Garcia Girls Lost Their Accents*. In our discussions of what it means to be American, there is so much talk of the importance of the self, and the very American idea that we can change our identity at any time—isn't that partly the fuel of the American Dream, the idea that we can be born into one identity but can grow up to shape another? Back in the 1920s, F. Scott Fitzgerald was already wondering if the American Dream was over; so, we wonder together, my students and I, what meaning the American Dream has for us now. How does living in America shape our identities? What relevance do any of these discussions have for American teenagers living in the twenty-first century? Or for me, their teacher?

Northerner. Lesbian.

Christian. Black. White.

Only child. Girl. Jock. Introvert.

Telling stories, I understood early on, is how we make sense of the world, or at least how I make sense of the world. Like all art, our stories reflect back to us some fundamental view of ourselves and the world, transformed and shaped into a thing of beauty and wonder. This is what I want to transmit to my students, the power of art in our lives, the power to transform our lives into art and beauty. This is the struggle, then—helping kids see why art matters, why they matter, why their lives, full of messiness and heartache and difficulties and joy, are the very stories they are both reading and writing. Being a teacher in the South, I realize, isn't so very different from being a teacher anywhere, gay or otherwise. The struggles are fundamentally the same, but it is my fervent hope that as we continue growing and learning, we continue to provide the space for all students to safely learn—and teach—these lessons.

7

Saving My Voice

Andrea Fazel

LAW AND GOVERNMENT TEACHER
NP3 Charter High School
Sacramento, California

During the first seven years of my teaching career, I lost my voice on a regular basis. At least twice a year, I would find myself physically unable to speak, reliant on the whiteboard and a loud student to convey the day's lessons. Far more often than that, I would find myself voiceless on another level.

I came out in the early 1990s, during my first year of college, not long after I had determined that I wanted to become a high school teacher. I imagined myself in the classroom, idealistic and inspiring, much like the central teacher in *Dead Poets Society*. Thoughts of being out in the classroom simply didn't come up, as though it was not only impossible but irrelevant to my future career. As I navigated through my college years, I focused on learning how to be my authentic self with a close circle of people, and gave little thought to the value of projecting my voice—being out in order to make my voice heard or my life more visible. In the midst of Queer Nation and ACT UP, attending one of the most LGBT-friendly campuses in the nation, UC Santa Cruz, my voice remained quietly focused inward.

When I began my teaching credential program a few years later, I had come to understand that my sexual orientation would present a challenge to my career plans. No one ever told me this. No one had to. After all, if being a gay teacher wasn't a big deal, I'd have known some, right? (Years later, I learned that at least a few of my teachers were gay, but that only reaffirmed my unspoken understanding that to be an openly gay teacher, even in the San Francisco Bay Area, was not a realistic option.)

On the first day of the program, we were instructed to introduce ourselves by sharing a poster that represented who we were—these posters would hang in the room for the coming year. My first worry, then, was what to share about myself in this professional setting. Ultimately, I chose to share my voice in a quiet way, incorporating an ACLU advertisement from the *Advocate* about LGBT equality. While I was tentative and a bit nervous, the stakes didn't feel particularly high yet. The real test would come in the classroom with my students. This self-revelation to a roomful of strangers opened a small door for me, helping me to quickly identify classmates who were also gay, as well as those who were ardent allies. Though I found supportive attitudes among my peers and my instructors, no one was able to provide resources that would help me find my voice in the classroom as a gay teacher.

As the year went on, it became my responsibility to educate my peers (and my instructors) about issues pertaining to LGBT students, and to educate myself on these same issues. I studied the Briggs Initiative—a failed proposition that would have made being gay (or supporting the rights of gay people) cause for termination for all public school teachers in California. I taught myself about early court cases filed by educators who were fired for being gay. At this point, I encountered the first edition of *One Teacher in Ten*, as well as a few other works pertaining to the experiences of LGBT educators. I read them all, hungry for any clue as to how to proceed in my teaching career. Unfortunately, the voices that emerged in those texts either seemed fictional to me (no one could ever be *that* out!) or reaffirmed what I had assumed: I had to be *very* careful—and very quiet.

The day I met my master teacher for my yearlong student-teaching placement was a powerful example of luck. Beth was a highly regarded teacher, and she became an invaluable mentor to me. I remember meeting with her for the first time in her classroom and spotting a poster covered with historical and literary figures with the caption "Unfortunately, history set the record a little too straight." My assumption was that I had been fortunate enough to be placed with a visible ally. I decided to let my voice come out in a small whisper, mentioning to her that my partner's father also taught in the district. She looked startled, but then told me that her partner also taught at that same school. I was stunned to learn that I had been placed with a mentor who was a lesbian!

During that year, we didn't talk much about the complexities of being gay teachers. I remember sharing brief anecdotes with her when the issue bubbled to the surface, but as she wasn't out to students at the school, I followed her lead and also kept my personal life carefully separate from my work life. From Beth, I learned that being a visible ally to students was critically important but that I might be able to do this without taking the risk of sharing my personal life with them.

Throughout the year, I struggled to be the teacher my students deserved while silencing my own voice. On the first day, one student looked me dead in the eye, slowly raised his notebook to reveal a rainbow flag, and lowered it again. I was startled to see how bold he was, and wondered if he was signaling that he had me figured out as well. Months later, he wrote an essay in which he came out to me; I came out to him in a private conversation, all the while making sure he understood that this was not common knowledge, and that I would appreciate him not sharing this information. Today, I wonder what model of voice I provided for him that year. Does he remember me as the student teacher who actually came out to him in 1996? Or does he look back and see me the way I saw the gay teachers in my past: as someone who could have modeled a path in the world as an out and proud gay person, but who failed in some way?

When I began my full-time teaching career, I had to figure out what my voice would sound like in my new school. As before, I hoped for mentors who could model their own path to finding their voice. On the first day, I saw a teacher who set off my "gaydar" immediately. When I learned she was a member of my department, I sought out her friendship. Later in the fall, Anne and I were talking privately, and she started the ball rolling:

"So, being gay at this school . . ." (Neither of us had explicitly come out to the other at this point.)

She proceeded to share her observations and lessons learned through her first ten years in education. "The people we hang out at lunch with," she said, "they are safe to be out to. But whatever you do, don't tell the guys who eat in the staff room. They're total homophobes."

I don't remember whether we even discussed the prospect of being out to students, but I doubt it.

All year I had struggled to figure out how to present myself. Were my body language, wardrobe, and voice not feminine enough? Was I too obvious? Were my fears of being discovered evident to the freshmen I tried and often failed to control each day? Did my internal struggles make me appear fearful and weak to my students?

One of the most vivid memories I have from my first year of teaching came late in the spring. One student in particular, Michael, was a difficult student for me. By this time, he was failing my class beyond all hope of repair, and he attended class only every few days. But when my wife met me on campus to pick me up from work one day, he was there to loudly say to his friend, "Hey, did you see that dyke on the *Ellen* show last night?" (The coming-out episode of *Ellen* had aired the night before.)

At least, I think that's what he said. I remember the laughter more.

It was clear both to me and to my wife that he was baiting me in some respect, and as we walked by, I looked off into the distance in front of me, pretending I didn't hear a word.

I was terrified.

I shared this with Anne, and she marched me into the office of a discipline administrator to share what had occurred. Together, they agreed that Michael didn't need to be in my class, and he was transferred into study hall for the remainder of the year. To my knowledge, this schedule change was not explained to him, beyond the fact that he had no mathematical chance to pass English at that point. At the time, I was simply grateful that I was being protected. Today, I am stunned that in the push to protect me, this opportunity to educate a student was so easily avoided.

The following year, I moved to another part of California so that my wife could complete her own credential program. I landed in a school that was conservative and large, and I knew I would probably leave within a year. It was clear to me that no matter what I might want to do, I would need to keep silent that year, and that there was no point in seeking allies among my colleagues. One student repeatedly asked me if I was married. Each time, it seemed that she sensed this would rattle me, and she would ask with a smirk on her face.

Each time, I deflected the question.

My wife and I had just had a commitment ceremony the summer before we moved, and every denial of our union chipped away at my sense of self a little more and made what voice I still possessed weaker still.

I don't remember the names of any of my colleagues from that year; I spent my lunches in my room almost every day, alone at first, but eventually joined by a handful of drama students. One student in particular, Laura, struck me from the moment I met her. I thought she might come out in the next few years. But her talk of her fiancé and her plans to join the military made me wonder if I had just jumped to conclusions.

At the end of the year, I knew that I would be moving back to Santa Cruz, and she was going to be stationed nearby. She spoke of staying in touch. The thought of the closet extending further into my home life repelled me, and I decided that I needed to come out to her.

"Yeah, we kind of wondered."

Wait . . . *we*?

"All of us who hung out in your room at lunch." I was startled by this revelation, and touched that it so clearly didn't bother them— that they saw me as the drama teacher they liked and respected and weren't distracted by the fact that I was gay.

Within a year, Laura had come out herself and was ultimately discharged from the military under Don't Ask, Don't Tell. When this widened conflict within her family, she ended up moving in with us for several months. I hope that from me she saw a possible path forward, having a voice that was authentic and strong. But given how I was navigating the closet at the time, I know that, at the least, I was sending very mixed messages.

Upon returning to Santa Cruz, I continued the pattern set the year before, living far from school, so that I could go to the store with my wife without worrying about bumping into my students or their parents. I carved out a small space where I didn't have to be silent, as long as I was nowhere near my job. I returned to the school where I had started. I continued to micromanage my image, always worrying about how I moved, how I sounded, what I said about my life. I continued to deflect questions about marriage, rationalizing to myself that technically, I wasn't married, so I wasn't really lying when I denied the most central relationship in my life.

All the while, I grew more and more depressed about my career. I had good days, good moments, but on the whole, I hated teaching and resented my students. In my mind, I placed the blame for my self-imposed silence on my students. By this time, I was no longer willing to be out to the students who came out to me, even as I was in charge of facilitating a support group for LGBT students through our counseling center. My silence had extended so far that I doubt many students would have seen me as any kind of ally.

In 2000, my second year back at the school, I made a decision: if I made it past the pink-slip date, I would come out to my students. It was the only way I could imagine being able to stay in the classroom for another year.

I carefully covered all my bases. I talked to my department chair, Lisa. She and I saw eye to eye on very little. She was old-school in every sense—Warriner's grammar books took up prime shelf space in her room, student papers bled with her red ink, and her wardrobe was always impeccably polished. When I told her what I wanted to do and why, she simply responded, "I just don't understand why you haven't done it before now. It's clearly killing you."

I met with our union representative. Evan told me that, to his knowledge, no teacher had ever come out in the district before, but that the bargaining agreement was very clear in banning discrimination on the basis of sexual orientation. He insisted that he and the union had my back. And he believed that our principal would be fine with it as well, so the union wouldn't need to be involved anyway.

When I met with the principal, the meeting wasn't quite so positive.

ME: "I'd like to come out to my students in the context of a lesson I am doing."

HER: "I can't tell you not to . . ."

ME: "That's right, you can't." (To this day, I have no idea where I found the nerve to say this aloud. I sometimes wonder if I just thought it loudly in my own head, but stayed silent.)

HER: "But I think you would be making a huge mistake."

She went on to warn me of the dangers: I would develop significant classroom management problems. Parents would call to complain and would want to pull their kids out of my class and out of the special program I taught. And she insisted that she didn't see the point, anyway, because teachers didn't have any reason to talk about their private lives with students.

I decided that, despite my principal's lack of support, I would proceed as planned. Soon after the pink-slip deadline, my sophomore English class would be starting to read *To Kill a Mockingbird*. I chose this class carefully because it was a special program that helped to build a tight-knit community. Plus, two students in the class talked openly of gay family members whom they loved dearly.

For the previous several years, as an opening to the novel, I had facilitated a discussion with my students about stereotypes, prejudice, and discrimination. We would discuss group identities, identify stereotypes about those identities, deconstruct them, and analyze the consequences of stereotypes. We would begin with a relatively innocuous category, such as cheerleaders. Then we would explore stereotypes about Latinos, a group that most of the students in the class belonged to. As we discussed these stereotypes, we would talk about the ways in which the stereotypes were untrue, and we would identify the ways in which those stereotypes, if believed, could lead to discriminatory behavior from others.

Every year, the third group that students chose was gay people. Every year my heart would race, fearing that I would suddenly become the direct focus of the conversation. As the list of stereotypes grew, it would become evident that they were focusing on stereotypes about gay men. I would ask, "Okay, are these stereotypes true of all gay men?" A room full of teenagers would nod their heads.

"Let me see if I've got this: Not all cheerleaders are airheads. Not all Latinos speak Spanish. But all gay men sleep around? Help me out here." Silence.

"Okay, let's try this another way. Raise your hand if you have a close friend or family member who is gay." About one-fourth of the class raised their hands. "All right, now only you get to answer my question: Are these stereotypes true of all gay men?"

"No. My uncle's gay, and he and his partner have been together forever!"

"No. I have a gay cousin, and he's totally macho!"

I would pause and then ask, "So how did the rest of you know how to answer, if you don't actually know gay people?" "The media," they would tell me.

I was going to do the same lesson again, only this time, I was going to finish it right.

After we discussed all three groups, I said, "Okay, now let me tell you about an example of how stereotypes can lead to prejudice, how prejudice can lead to discrimination, and how that can actually affect a person's life." I went on to tell them about "a teacher I know who is gay." Every detail I shared about whispered comments, lewd remarks carved into furniture, pain and fear born of silence came directly from my experience. They asked questions about "this teacher" and shared their outrage that she would be treated this way. Finally, I told them that I was talking about myself.

The room was silent. I could hear my own heart beating.

Tom raised his hand. I didn't know him well yet, but every stereotype in my head was setting off alarm bells. He was a star football player, high status, and exactly the "kind of kid" I assumed would cause trouble for me.

"Yes, Tom?"

"Did you say that we're the first class you ever shared this with?"

I nodded.

"Then we should feel pretty special."

The class applauded.

We talked for a few minutes more, and I answered a few more questions.

"Were you nervous?" I showed them my shaking hands and pointed out that I was still leaning against the bookcase for a reason.

"Wait, you've been with your partner for *how* long?" This was, for many of my students, the real shocker. My wife and I had been together for eight years, an eternity for a sophomore.

One student, clearly seeking to protect me, warned the rest of the class, "Nobody better tell anyone!"

I smiled. "Do you honestly think I would have told a room full of sophomores this if I wanted it to stay secret?" We all laughed. And then we moved on, back to the novel.

To my knowledge, no parent called to complain. The walls didn't come tumbling down. Nothing happened.

Except everything happened. I remember feeling instantly lighter and younger. More free. I didn't talk much at school about being gay, but when it was relevant, I did. More than anything, I stopped feeling like I needed to constantly look over my shoulder. And for the first time I felt comfortable letting my authentic personality come through in interactions with my students. For the first time I was able to let go and just focus on teaching.

Another year passed, and an opportunity to move to a new school arose, one that my wife had worked at for a few years, where I knew the staff and where I thought I might be energized by a more creative teaching environment. The tradeoff? The principal was new, conservative, religious, and ambivalent about having me there.

Back in the closet I went for the next two years, out only to a select group of colleagues, anonymous to the rest. I was sure that no other option was available to me, given the nature of our school community and the principal's leadership style—at least, not until I was tenured again. In that time, I never came out to a single student. My voice faded again. Before long, my depression about teaching returned, and I walked away two years later, going to law school, determined never to return to the classroom.

And yet . . .

Throughout law school, my interest in education never faded. I looked into the rights of LGBT students in schools and wrote about the first amendment rights of LGBT teachers. I sought out internships that would put me in the offices of people fighting for LGBT teachers, Gay-Straight Alliances, and LGBT parents. Afterward, I landed in an organization that worked to train educators and students to create safe and inclusive learning environments for all students, regardless of sexual orientation or gender identity and expression.

I would conduct staff trainings on state laws regarding the rights of LGBT students, and share stories of my own years in the classroom. I advocated best practices that I had rarely implemented as a teacher. I played the part of someone whose voice was strong and confident, all the while remembering how meek my voice had been. I would watch teachers and administrators work together to create the kind of school environment I had never had the opportunity to experience, and I realized that some of my old wounds were gradually healing. I would grow wistful, wondering what it would have been like to work in such an environment. Six years into my post-teaching life, I found that I really missed teaching. I realized the problem wasn't teaching. It was my willingness to let others dictate the teacher I would be, what my voice would sound like.

I needed to set some ground rules for what "Teaching Career 2.0" would look like for me. I had to be out from day one. By this point, a

Google search would settle that question anyway. Being closeted was no longer an option, even if I thought I could stomach it. But I knew that silencing myself had been one of the biggest factors driving me out of teaching, and I owed it to myself to see what would happen if I didn't voluntarily give up my voice.

Through a friend, I learned about a small charter school in my neighborhood that she thought might be a good fit for me. I was skeptical, to say the least. I live in Sacramento, in a neighborhood where "Yes on Prop 8" signs and stickers had littered yards and cars in every direction. I found it hard to imagine that this would be a place where my voice would be welcome, let alone safe. But I was curious, and I reached out to the administration at NP3 High School.

When I met the administrators, I had a bit of a chip on my shoulder. I tested them. When asked why I wanted to return to teaching, I mentioned my partner, and what *she* was doing in the field of education. I watched their expressions for any sign of tension. None came. Instead, they both quickly moved to selling me on what a diverse and safe environment the school was. I was, frankly, confused. Here were two administrators, both coming from deeply religious backgrounds (both had previously worked together at a Catholic school), clearly wanting me at their school in part *because* I was gay. When the job offer came, I went for it.

When I started at NP3, I was, to say the least, nervous.

Setting up my classroom was my first real test of my new voice. Would I be afraid to put a picture of my wife on my desk? I debated how to handle this and ultimately put up a collage of pictures, most of which included my wife but also our dogs, our nephew, and other important people in my life. The pictures became an entry point into those earliest coming-out discussions with students that year. A student would ask, "Where was that picture taken?" "Paris." "Oh, did you like it?" And we'd continue the conversation without discussion of the fact that the picture in question showed my wife and me with our arms around each other in front of the Eiffel Tower. Eventually, someone asked who she was, and I simply answered, "My wife." The conversation then continued on without complication. I have never done a "very special lesson" again. Coming out to my students happens organically, and many know through word of mouth. Each time it happens, I feel my heart race a bit, but I have yet to regret speaking honestly.

In the spring of my first year at NP3, we held a Day of Silence. We modified the cards typically used for Day of Silence, adding the phrase "Because at NP3, we don't have to be silent." That day, about 20 percent of our students participated in the Day of Silence; I joined them. Just at the moment I was finding my voice, I came to see the power in voluntarily giving it up for the day. I started each class with a poem I had written, projecting it onto the screen in lieu of speaking. In part, it reads:

> Today, I am silent to honor the sacrifices I have made along the way
> to finding my own voice.

> . . . I am silent to ensure
> That I never take for granted the power
> Of my own voice.

> Today, I am silent only by choice.

Today, my students and their parents know that I am a lawyer who never practiced law a day in her life, that I have two incredibly cute dogs, and that my sarcastic sense of humor only thinly hides a very sentimental heart. They know my wife, and they talk about how sweet she is. They know that I am passionate about teaching, passionate about the government and law classes I teach, and passionately committed to the needs of my students. The fact that I am openly gay is just another piece of data for most of them. For some, it is a critical piece of data that has helped them navigate their own coming-out experience or has prepared them to better support a friend who was coming out. For others, my presence has provided a counterpoint to deeply held religious beliefs, as they learn to express their views and ask questions respectfully, rather than feeling entitled to express those views as a weapon against me or against their peers.

I am finally experiencing the joy of teaching the way I always imagined it would be: building personal and intellectual connections with my students, watching them grow and develop, laughing with them at the utter randomness of high school students, and being fully myself every step of the way.

I am now in the sixth year of my new life as an openly gay teacher. I wonder how my teaching career would have evolved differently if I could have seen this version of myself in the classroom when I was twenty-two years old. I suspect it would have changed everything. I look back at the rare moments when I did open myself up to risks, and I see with the wisdom of hindsight that none of the terrible things I feared ever came to pass. Instead, my greatest moments of pain came when I acted on my mistaken belief that my silence would save me.

There are those who believe that unresolved emotional distress manifests itself in the body. For me, losing my voice was both literal and metaphorical in those first seven years of teaching. Since my return to teaching, I have yet to lose my voice now that I am unwilling to sacrifice it.

8

Two Teachers in Twenty

Elisa Waters

SPANISH TEACHER
Jericho Middle School
Jericho, New York

Joey Waters

ENGLISH TEACHER
Cold Spring Harbor High School
Cold Spring Harbor, New York

"Ms. Waters and the Other Ms. Waters." That was what one student participant wrote on his or her evaluation form next to "Name of presenter(s)." It was 2009 and we were running a workshop at an LGBT conference. Those names have stuck.

Thankfully, our stories of coming out, getting married, having children, and being teachers are not ones filled with angst. In fact, when most people meet us and our children, they are less taken aback by our family dynamic than with what it is we each teach: one of us is a Spanish teacher; the other, English. This begs the humorous question: what happens during an argument? Does one of you launch into Spanish and is the other a sesquipedalian? We will keep you guessing.

Our districts sit about fifteen minutes apart on the North Shore of Long Island, and for all the similarities and differences between our two environments, what stands out for both of us is how our coming out has affected those around us in ways we never quite anticipated. Before coming out, our heads swirled with thoughts about what this would mean for us as individuals and as a couple, for our family, and for our careers. We thought of conversations we had with educators who had decades of life experience on us—and the stories of life in the closet or life with just barely a foot out the door. Some of these teachers spoke to us about being gay only behind closed doors and with whispers, the same foreboding tone that was once used when people spoke about cancer. We read books such as *One Teacher in Ten*, which told us about the possible benefits and the potential pitfalls of being out in an educational environment. We thought of the images the mirrors tossed back at us every morning, and we knew we had to risk it and hope that we were living in a time and were part of school communities that were ready to accept this aspect of our whole selves. After all, how could we encourage our students to be their authentic selves if we couldn't do the same?

The year 2008 marked my fifteenth year teaching in the United States and the first time I would share something with my class I had never had occasion to utter before. During a health unit in my middle-school Spanish class, we were reviewing vocabulary with a Smart Board lesson—defining vocabulary, answering questions, offering diagnoses—and one of the slides said "*La profesora está embarazada.*" I asked my students, "¿Qué significa la frase?" After numerous guesses, including the most obvious one, as this word is a false cognate to English, one student said, "I think that means 'The teacher is pregnant.'" Next came the pregnant pause as the reality of that statement sunk in. In what felt like a slow-motion candid-camera moment, each student leaned in ever so slightly, stared at my stomach, and smiled. As the enthusiasm swelled, I shared that my partner and I were expecting our first child in June. Then came the thunderous applause and the sound of chairs sliding back as students rose from their seats with shouts of joy and suggestions for baby names. It turned out that teaching Spanish provided the perfect segue for me to come out— both about being pregnant and being married to a woman. That was more than six years ago.

⁓

June 4, 2008. The nervous energy of my tenth-grade Honors English students was beginning to make me anxious; I knew they were ready for the final exam that was only days away, but I also knew I had to tell them I might be absent at any point. They were feeling the pressure of the test and I was feeling the pressure of a life-altering event, telling my students I was gay, married, and expecting a child. I failed in delivering this news yesterday, the only time I have ever choked in front of a class. It had to be today. With sweaty palms, another first, I told my students, "I might be absent at some point in the next few days or on the day you take your final. I don't want you to worry if I am; you are ready for your final, and I am going to be out for a good reason: my partner and I are expecting our first child." Students started to clap, some students had to lean over and explain to their peers what I meant by *partner*, and then those students, too, started to clap. The class ended with a standing ovation.

We often comment on the fact that it isn't as though we came out once and then never had to do it again. We come out on a regular basis. Just the other day one of us was calling to make a doctor's appointment for the other and there it was, yet again, a moment of sharing our relationship status and sexual orientation with a stranger on the other end of the phone. Sometimes we think that this is what it means to be gay in the twenty-first century; we simply keep on coming out. As educators we come out each year to a new batch of students, only now the surprise we feel is when students don't know we are gay and hear it first when we share a story that involves our family and is linked to the curriculum. Now we assume word about our family has traveled, but again, when you are part of the norm, you are not the talk of the town; it is nice to blend.

What we didn't know when we came out at our respective schools is that we would open the floodgates to our peers sharing their own coming-out stories, sometimes about themselves, but largely about their children, siblings, aunts and uncles, nieces and nephews, cousins, and friends. In the years since we stood in front of our classes, countless colleagues have come forward and confided in us about where they are in their coming-out journey. One colleague went from sharing concerns about her child's sexual orientation in hushed tones to boasting about her child's wedding day on Facebook; others have shared worries and questions about how to help their children come out in ways that are positive and not self-destructive; and still others simply want to hear what challenges we have faced in being out and how they can help the person in their life feel good about who he or she is. One moment that is particularly memorable is when one friend and colleague, in a moment of panic, introduced her wife as the nanny of their children; figuring out how to be out isn't always easy. We believe, though, that sharing our stories has helped others find their voices—voices we would never have known were silent.

When we reflect on our coming-out experiences, we realize that in many ways it is not so much about us as individuals but is really about us as members of respective communities. When a student moved into one of our districts and was chatting with her new peers and learning about her new school, something came up about Ms. Waters being gay. She was taken aback and said, "You shouldn't say that. Why would you say that?" The students smiled, and one quickly pointed to a photo on the board and said, "Because there she is with her wife and kids. She *is* gay." These students weren't using the word *gay* in a derogatory tone; they were using the word in a factual statement. We have helped normalize the idea of having a teacher in the district who identifies as gay, but those around us have sometimes been the ones who opened our eyes to the power of language.

We both used to use the term *partner* all the time when referring to the other. It was a term we were both comfortable with, and we felt it offered a good definition of our relationship: we were partners in marriage and partners in parenthood. It wasn't until I was talking to a parent about Thanksgiving plans that I rethought my own vocabulary. I said that my partner and I were going to my in-laws. She looked at me and said, "Why don't you just call her your wife?" She made it seem like the most obvious statement in the world. She was casual in her tone, and it was almost as though it struck her as silly, not funny silly but illogically silly, that I would use a term different from other married people. I taught my community and they were teaching me in return.

Hearing the words "Do you have a minute?" now sounds like a secret password whenever someone utters the phrase and it is addressed to me. In theory, that could kick-start an infinite number of conversations, but more often than not it is code for "I want to come out to you." We have had more than one parent out him- or herself to us. We believe those parents felt safe confiding something many of us view as personal, because we are open about that aspect of who we are.

Just as parents use that colloquial turn of phrase, so have many students who have crossed my path.

Our students coming out to us is sometimes humorous, such as one student saying, just as she was about to walk on stage for an event, "Ms. Waters, I want to tell you I'm bisexual," to heart-wrenching, tear-drenched moments of, "Ms. Waters, I can't be gay. I just can't. I know I am, but my family will hate me; this goes against everything we are," to the angst-filled, "Umm, I think I might be gay." My personal favorite was one young man who said, after an upbeat conversation about being gay, "Where have you been all my life?" He was seventeen.

What these same students don't know, and what we often wonder about, is how many students sit before us every day and go home to messages that promote hate or intolerance, foster humor at the expense of others, or condone derogatory language? I can clearly recall one incident after our son was born, when the family of a young person I tutored learned of the birth of our child and our status as same-sex parents and never contacted me again. We have both heard through the grapevine unverified rumors of parents (granted, a small percentage of them) who asked not to have their child in our classes because we identify as gay. It's never stopped us from pursuing our goal of creating classroom environments that are safe and inclusive for every learner and also appropriate for who we are as teachers and as people. We share quick stories about our children and family, as they relate to the lesson, and promote respect and acceptance for everyone and everything the world has to offer. Our educational philosophy includes normalizing language, connecting history to current events, and exposing students to inclusive curriculum that reflects our global community. We hope that all this lends itself to a classroom community open to questioning, debating, and growing.

Our stories aren't filled with drama, and maybe that's the point. We are what the statistics say: two parents, two children, two dogs, and a fence around the yard. Perhaps that is how we know that as a society we are making strides in respecting and acknowledging that individuals who identify in a way that challenges the societal majority are also part of the bell curve of normal now, or at least that's the case in the communities of which we are a part.

Maybe more to the point is the following anecdote. It is a Friday night in mid-October: we—the two of us, our kids, and a couple of gay and trans-identified youth who have become part of our extended family—are gathered around our dining room table passing food back and forth like the modern-day Waltons. How we all self-identify in this circle is as varied as the permutations of letters in the alphabet, but what matters most is what one of the young individuals around the table says: "I can't believe your life is like this. I want this. I want to bring my mom here to see your family and to know that *this* life is possible for me and that I can be happy, and gay."

PART 2

Unexpected Journeys

9

A Mother's Journey

Susan Fitzpatrick Radzilowski

RETIRED SCHOOL SOCIAL WORKER
Detroit Public Schools
Detroit, Michigan

My son is transgender. The day he was born, twenty-four years ago, was the happiest day of my life. After twenty-four difficult hours of labor I was given a general anesthetic, and he was delivered by emergency Cesarean. Later that evening I was awakened in the recovery room by a nurse exclaiming, "Congratulations. You have given birth to a beautiful baby girl!" I was overcome with joy.

I embraced parenting my "daughter" with enthusiasm and delight. Being a new mother was a lot of work, but it was exciting too. What fun it was to see the world through the eyes of a child! I was astounded by the depth of my love for my child.

I was a single mom when my "daughter" was little, and I worked full time. Fortunately, my employment as school social worker enabled me to stay home with "her" during the summer months. I took full advantage of this time with my child. I loved spending those warm, sunny days together. Free of the boundaries imposed by work and school, our afternoons were made up of zoo trips, berry picking, reading, crafts, baking, horseback riding, and camping trips. Sometimes we would get up early and ride our bikes to a doughnut shop for breakfast. When Alex was five I took out a loan, and we got a brand new popup camper. We took it to local campgrounds and even slept in it in our driveway a couple of times.

Alex was a good kid—kind, obedient, curious, and eager to please. "She" was a good student too—hard working, diligent, and creative. In fourth grade Alex took up the violin and over time became an accomplished musician. I used to love to listen to "her" practice the violin. When Alex was nine we joined a mother-daughter book club, which we faithfully attended each month for the next four years.

Alex and I used to love spending days exploring nearby little towns, cider mills, and bike trails. We called our special outings adventures, because these day trips were to places that were new to us. Occasionally, when Alex and I were having one of our adventures, I would stop and consciously breathe in the moment. I wanted to commit these shared experiences permanently into my memory—the sights, the sounds, the senses. I knew that "her" childhood would fly by, that this treasured time was brief.

I'll never forget the night Alex told me "she" thought "she" was a boy. "She" was fifteen years old and in the tenth grade. It was past midnight and the two of us were sitting together on the living room sofa. Sobbing, with a face flushed redder than I had ever seen, Alex confided, "I need to tell you something, Mom." After a long pause I heard these words: "I think I am a boy. I am afraid I am transgender." I was surprised—shocked, actually—but I managed to remain outwardly calm and encouraged Alex to share "her" feelings.

That night Alex told me everything. Some of "her" words are seared into my memory: "I have felt this way for a long time." "I am a freak." "I want to kill myself." When I heard these words, I was scared.

Alex and I talked deep into the night. We held hands, and I listened and comforted "her." I was able to get Alex to promise not to act on "her" impulse to hurt or kill "herself." I reassured "her" that the family would be there always—"she" would not be left to struggle with these feelings alone. It was a sacred promise that I have kept to this day.

When we finally went to bed in the middle of the night, both of us were physically and mentally exhausted. The next day I allowed Alex to miss school to catch up on "her" sleep after such a difficult night. "She" slept in until noon. Around lunchtime I opened the bedroom door to check on "her." I saw that Alex was lying calmly, reading a book, in the upper bunk bed. "She" seemed serene and peaceful. I approached "her" with an embrace and a tender hug. "I will always be here for you, honey. No matter what," I reminded gently. "I am your mother and you are my daughter, and that is all that matters." "No, Mom," Alex replied. "I am your son." I did not let on at the time, but that bold, affirmative statement shocked me. The degree of confidence with which Alex claimed his maleness was unexpected and startling.

Alex began his gender transition from female to male with breathtaking speed. I had expected a period of questioning before he acted on his feelings and was unprepared when he immediately decided upon a new name, a boy's name: Liam. Next he asked me to buy him some boxer shorts and a suit.

In his desire to appear more masculine, Liam began binding his chest with elastic bandages. He would wrap two or three bandages around his chest to project a more masculine profile. This practice is common in female-to-male transgender teens, but it can lead to serious health problems, like bruised and deformed ribs, slowed blood flow to the lymph nodes, damaged muscles, and blood clots. As I learned, compression shirts do not have the health complications that are associated with elastic bandages. We found a resource online and I purchased several compression shirts for him.

During that first year of Liam's transition, most of my energy was focused on supporting him emotionally. My husband (Liam's stepfather) and I arranged for Liam to start a course of therapy. The goal of the therapy was not to "repair" or "correct" his gender identity but to help him explore his sense of self in a safe place. To that end, Liam saw a licensed psychologist at least once a week for the next two years. We also consulted regularly with both pastors from our Lutheran church, his school counselor, a gender specialist, and his pediatrician. Arranging for these services was time consuming and expensive but well worth it. I felt I needed the guidance and counsel of experts in the area. In fact, this consultation proved invaluable and helped reduce my anxiety and increased my confidence as a parental decision maker.

Even though my support of Liam was unwavering, saying good-bye to my "daughter" hurt like nothing before or since. I felt lonely, having no other parents of transgender youth to share my feelings with. I went to one PFLAG (Parents and Friends of Lesbians and Gays) meeting, but that was a disaster. As a first-time visitor I was placed in a group with other "new" parents. The other moms and dads were sharing their feelings about having a lesbian or gay son or daughter. It seemed that other parents had come to accept their gay child by reminding themselves that their son or daughter was still the same person. But my child had a new name, a new gender identity, and a new appearance with more changes to come. Was he still the same person? It did not feel like it. I broke down in the meeting in inconsolable tears.

As the years passed I would come to realize that Liam was indeed the same person, despite his new name and gender identity. I realized that he and I could (and did!) retain our special connection and shared history regardless of his gender transition. But in these first difficult months I did not yet realize this, and my sense of loss was overwhelming.

More devastating than my feelings about losing my "daughter," though, were my fears of losing Liam to suicide. Early on in his transition, Liam had expressed suicidal feelings. I developed a persistent sense of foreboding about Liam's emotional well-being that remains even to this day. Eager to learn more about issues facing the transgender community, I devoured books and research studies on transgender issues and even attended conferences focusing on LGBT issues. I learned that nearly half of young transgender people have seriously considered taking their lives and that one-quarter report having made a suicide attempt.

The reality of transgender suicide hit home when a young transgender friend of Liam's took his own life. The young man was bright and from a supportive family. He was a lot like Liam. His death still haunts me.

By the time Liam was a high school senior he was living full time as a boy. He came out widely at school as transgender about six months into his transition. We were so fortunate—his classmates and teachers were mostly supportive. Every adult at his school embraced his new name, and all of his teachers addressed Liam using male pronouns. Several teachers even reached out to Liam personally, offering to help and support in any way possible. I am grateful to this day for the care shown to Liam, and to me, by extension.

In addition to widespread support at school, our faith community continued to embrace Liam with the love they had always shown him. Most of our relatives and family friends were supportive too. My parents, who were in their seventies, surprised and pleased me with their willingness to accept Liam's gender transition. They love Liam dearly and were concerned only about his welfare. We had several long talks in which they asked a lot of questions. They showed their support for Liam by using his new name and accepting his male gender identity. A few of our relatives obstinately clung to Liam's old name and insisted on using feminine pronouns with reference to Liam. Their stubbornness stung.

When Liam was seventeen, I allowed him to petition the court to legally change his first name. As a result, his high school diploma, when received the following June, would reflect his chosen name. This would enable Liam to enter adulthood with his legal and social identity in alignment, thus avoiding confusion with regard to his legal, educational, and employment status. I had no misgivings about this decision.

Permitting Liam to begin taking testosterone was a difficult choice for me to make. I knew that irreversible physical changes would occur once he began to take testosterone. He would begin to grow facial hair and his voice would deepen. The thought of these changes unsettled me. A greater concern though was about potential adverse health consequences from the testosterone.

Another barrier was that we had difficulty finding a doctor who would oversee testosterone treatment for a minor. Liam was not quite eighteen years old. After struggling to find a doctor we could trust and relate to, I discovered that my warm, caring family physician also treated transgender patients with hormone therapy. I was a fairly new patient to her practice, but Dr. "M" had won my trust and confidence with her genuine concern and interest in my life. On my first appointment with her two years earlier, she had spent more than ninety minutes with me, learning about my life and my concerns, and administering a thorough physical. Liam had not yet come out to me, so his gender transition was not a point of discussion during that visit.

When I noticed her advertisement on the web page of the local LGBT center, I immediately phoned her office and scheduled an appointment. Liam made a seamless transition from his pediatrician to Dr. M, and his hormone therapy began shortly thereafter. This was a big step for both of us, and having the services of a physician with whom I had an established positive relationship went a long way toward helping to alleviate my fears.

Soon after Liam started taking hormone injections, his appearance began to change. He became more muscular, and I saw the beginnings of facial hair. His voice deepened. He no longer resembled the androgynous teenager of a few years back. He was starting to look like a young man. The familiar sadness I had struggled with about losing the "daughter" I had raised began to bubble up anew. I kept my thoughts to myself, but it was difficult to watch this transformation. I had loved my "daughter" deeply, and it was a painful step in letting go of "her" and welcoming a son.

Some aspects of Liam's transition were heartbreaking for me. One of the most challenging tasks I faced was to balance my unconditional support for him with my feelings of loss at losing a cherished "daughter." At times, Liam, with his new name and masculine gender identity, seemed like an altogether different person. My sadness was magnified when he would give me awards, trophies, and other mementos from his childhood, saying, "Mom, I don't want this trophy anymore because this is not my name now. I know you will want to keep it, though." He tried to be tender with me on these occasions, using soft tones and kind gestures. Nevertheless, his words felt like a repudiation of his childhood that went beyond gender. Even though two years had passed, I continued to grieve privately. I kept my feelings to myself, fearing that expressing them might be construed as a lack of support for Liam. Each item Liam gave me I carefully placed in a box on the floor of my closet, and I began to acquire a hidden shrine for my "daughter" and our years together.

Nine years have passed. I no longer second-guess my decision to support my son in his gender transition. Liam has changed in many ways—and so have I. We have traveled together on a journey both difficult and triumphant. Our relationship has evolved over the years, but one constant remains—the enduring love between mother and child.

10

Gay and Brown
in Private Schools

Ashok Reddy

HISTORY TEACHER
Mainline Academy
Anytown, California

In the spring of 1985, my Indian, first generation immigrant parents—who, after several years of wandering, had decamped to the sleepy and relatively affluent New Jersey suburbs of New York City—approached me with the idea of going to private school.

I had no idea what this entailed. The suggestion seemed to come out of nowhere. But if I think back, there was some logic to it. Like many of their fellow immigrant friends, my parents tended to follow what other Indians they were acquainted with were doing. Most Indians they knew in the area (and in 1985 there weren't so many) had left large extended family and clan support structures behind when they moved to the United States after immigration laws had changed as a result of the Civil Rights Act of 1965. Bereft of that support, in a new country and trying to master new ways of being, they relied on each other for guidance. Partly out of social pressure created within the group and partly because their parents often didn't know of other options, it wasn't so unusual to suddenly see a slew of Indian kids taking classes at the same music school, attending the same summer camp, or applying to the same private school or college after one of us had chosen that route.

My mother was a physician. She worked with another Indian doctor at a small clinic they had set up in the Bronx eight years before. He had sent his son to a private school, and that was enough to compel my parents to do the same. I had also been tracked as a gifted kid up to that point, so sending me to a school where they thought my abilities would be matched with resources to put me on the path to a high-powered college wasn't necessarily an empty investment.

I don't remember much about when they first approached me with the idea, but I do remember that I wasn't that keen on it. Like most sixth graders, my life revolved around my friends, and they were all staying put and heading to the combined middle and high school in the very working-class, very Italian, and very undiverse town that we lived in. Despite the fact that I was the victim of overt and subtle racism, I, like many of my peers, wanted things in my life to remain uncomplicated. Why would I leave my friends to go to a school forty minutes away by bus?

But shortly after my parents' initial approach, fate intervened. My best friend at the time announced that his family was moving back to Japan that summer. I was a sensitive kid, so this development threw me for a loop. Suddenly uncertain about my future and probably a little off-kilter from feeling depressed about my friend's imminent departure, I remember feeling unmoored enough to at least be open to the possibility of trying something new. I agreed to visit the school.

Coincidentally, I had also taken up a new activity late that spring: I had started learning how to play tennis. On the school tour, the student tour guide pointed out the two rundown tennis courts, explaining that they were where the seventh-and-eighth-grade tennis team practiced (my town had no such team for middle schoolers). It felt like the stars had aligned to help make my decision. A few short weeks after my visit, the school sent my family a letter to say that I had been accepted. Without my best friend tying me to my town school and with aspirations of tennis greatness, I told my parents that I would go.

That fall I began the first of my six years at Green Meadows School in New Jersey.

Later, when friends in college asked about my time there, I remembered it as a generally positive experience. I faced none of the overt hostility that I had faced in grade school. When other students didn't seem to have an awareness of India or something that fell outside their mainstream view of American society, they at least seemed willing to learn. At GM I also developed and honed my love of history, and I had some memorable teachers who left lasting impressions on me. I experienced the successes and challenges that many kids my age experienced in a relatively safe environment surrounded by mostly high-achieving kids. And I played tennis throughout my years there.

Not until six years after I had graduated from high school and became a teacher myself did I recognize that the story below the surface of my time at GM was a more complicated one. Not until I had some distance from the situation did I begin to reflect on the impact these undercurrents had on me. In doing so, I remember coming to terms with feeling marginalized in a way I could not articulate when I actually attended the school.

In six years at GM I had one teacher of color—an art teacher in eighth grade. While my love of history was cultivated there, it began with a class unfortunately titled Third World Problems, the only history class offered in the high school that focused on non-Western history. And was it my imagination or did the History Department's only award go every year to a student who geeked out on World War I—specifically the European Theater? No student body president in my entire time there was a student of color. The only time students of color took center stage was during the Diversity Day festivities, which revolved around fashions shows and food festivals. And while a growing number of Korean, Indian, and other Asian families were sending their kids to GM, there were only four black students in my class of 120 kids, even though a sizable black population lived down the hill from the school.

If nothing else, I realized that I left GM with a sense of *otherness*—a sense that, while I could always look in, as a person of color I was never a full participant in the proceedings. The teachers and student leaders at the school never looked like me, and the images of people who looked like me in the "classic" education I was given were always sparse. Most troubling? It seemed that none of the adults in the community were bothered by this. If they, as adults I respected, didn't have a problem with it, why should I? But I did.

The other thing that time and distance allowed me to reflect on was what it was like for me to slowly realize in my last few years of high school that I might be gay.

I don't remember any out LGBT teachers at GM, although there were at least a few teachers on the faculty who many of us students thought might be gay—a fact that was confirmed during my later visits as an alum. The word *fag* was certainly casually thrown around as a slur by teenage boys, but I never felt or saw any deep menace in it. We also were no different than most other schools at the time in that we did not have a Gay-Straight Alliance. In retrospect I don't think it was surprising that I didn't fully embrace the idea that I was gay in high school—partly because there were so few adult role models to show what "being gay" would be like.

As is the case for many people, college was a time for me to grow into my identity as an LGBT person. I came out my freshman year and marched in Pride parades, participated in ACT UP demonstrations, and helped organize speakers almost from day one. I think of my college years as a time when being gay was my primary political minority identity. I still connected to my identity as an Indian—I had come to the university I attended because it had one of the most highly regarded South Asian studies departments in the country. But I never regarded being Indian or a person of color as a political identity during that time. Unlike the student LGBT group on campus, which focused on claiming public political space and championing acceptance and fair treatment, the Indian student groups focused on college versions of the fancy-dress shows and food extravaganzas that I had assiduously avoided in high school. I never went to a single Indian student group–sponsored gathering the whole time I was in college.

I had a serious boyfriend in 1996 when I got a job in Chicago helping supervise the after-school computer lab at an independent school (nondenominational private schools had by then pushed to rebrand themselves as "independent schools" to de-emphasize the exclusive reputation that clung to them). My other assigned duty was to support the seventh-grade teacher with his curriculum unit on India. At least part of the reason I got the job was because my boyfriend knew the out lesbian who was the head of the art department. I felt no need to worry about being out; and indeed this was the case after I started. It was my first time back on the campus of an independent school since I had graduated from high school five years before. I would eventually become a full-time teaching intern at the school the following year with my own classroom to manage.

There were certainly more out gay teachers at the school I now worked at than the one I had attended—two were even department chairs. There was less tolerance of gay slurs in the hallways. Teachers and even students newly empowered by gay-straight alliances stepped in to call perpetrators out. I had open, candid, mentoring conversations with questioning kids who found it easier to talk to me than the other older gay faculty because of my age. I credit the growth of national Gay, Lesbian, and Straight Education Network (GLSEN), which had one of its most active chapters in Chicago at the time, and the slowly changing cultural climate with helping bring about this change.

There was certainly more of a non–Western civilization presence in the school's curriculum than I had experienced at GM. The history department chair taught an elective class on South African history, another colleague taught an elective on the Middle East. Two of the elective classes I taught were Modern Asia and Global Religions. The English department had a similarly diverse set of elective offerings.

But, for a school in the middle of Chicago, it's interesting that I still had few colleagues of color on campus—if I remember correctly there were fewer teachers of color than there were gay teachers. I don't remember any of the positions of power in the student body or on the faculty being held by students or adults of color. And I still experienced a lingering feeling that the presence of people of color who looked like me, the stories and cultures we were connected to, and the nonwhite perspectives that we brought to our teaching craft were largely meant to add some spice to the life of the school, similar to the culture-day explosions I had experienced in high school. Everybody knew, for example, that the *important* humanities classes, the required ones, were grounded in Western civilizations and Western literature. The elective classes were regarded as fun explorations once you got the real learning out of the way. At times it felt as if I was reliving my marginalization experience at GM.

Sometimes I found myself having uncomfortable conversations with older, more experienced teachers that, to be kind, gave me pause. One teacher kept recounting that her favorite memory of her trip to India was of the faithful, humble servants they had in their employ, who had been so good at taking orders. Another pressed to know where my family was "really from" after I told the person I was a proud native of New Jersey. More than one teacher asked if I could speak "Indian" and seemed put out when I politely declined because it made me feel like I was performing an act.

But my identity as a gay teacher attracted no such curiosity or interest.

To its credit, the school sent some of my colleagues and me to a conference called the People of Color Conference (POCC), run by the national membership organization for independent schools. It had been set up to create a space where teachers of color could find affinity and support as they navigated independent school culture in which we were a distinct minority. At the outset I did not know what to expect. I had no idea at that point what a "person of color" was—I had never used that term before myself.

At the conference, I attended sessions about the impact of privilege and structural racism. I learned a new vocabulary to speak about the marginalization I had experienced in middle and high school and what I was continuing to experience as a teacher. I participated in discussions about what more diverse curriculums in independent schools could look like. There were movies about educational equity into the wee hours of the morning. I met hundreds of educators of color from across the country who also taught in independent schools. Many of them seemed to share the dual feeling of being connected to their schools while also feeling a disconnection that was hard to give voice to.

My experience at the conference was the genesis of my development as a politically aware teacher of color. I came back energized and elated to have some framework to reflect on the moments of discomfort I was having and the challenges that the families and students of color whom I worked with were experiencing as well.

It seemed strange to me that I felt no similar visceral reaction when I went to the national GLSEN conference the year before. It too had been well organized and well attended. The topics had focused similarly around empowerment as an underrepresented teacher. I felt extremely positive about what I learned and the connections I made with LGBT teachers around the country, but somehow the call to action as an LGBT teacher didn't reverberate in the same way as this newfound call to action as a teacher of color.

The truth was that I felt no dissonance or discomfort about being a gay teacher at my school. And this feeling was mirrored at each of the schools I would teach at.

When I was offered a full-time position teaching history the following year at a school in Washington, DC, I made a point to ask if there would be any issue with my being an out gay teacher. I was ready to say that I would be fine if they retracted the offer because the school was uncomfortable having a gay faculty member.

The head of the Humanities Department didn't even pause in replying, saying in the kindest voice possible, "I appreciate that you felt comfortable enough to tell me. But I don't think that you will find it to be an issue at our school."

In the three years I worked at the school, I never felt that my sexual orientation was a concern for any of my colleagues or any of the parents of my students. After some initial hesitation on my part about telling students I was gay (I had been told by friends who taught in public schools that you could be fired for doing so), it became an accepted fact on campus. We even had a short-lived, low-key, gay male teacher social group that met occasionally at each other's houses to watch the early seasons of *Queer as Folk*. I remember only one problematic conversation in that time. It occurred during a faculty meeting where a faculty member ignorantly conveyed that an effeminate-acting and attention-seeking gay boy in the middle school was bringing the harassment he was facing on himself by being "too loud." The other teachers and I made our displeasure known.

In 2001, when I was offered a job to help start a new school in Sonoma County, an hour north of San Francisco, I mentioned again to my future boss, after she made the offer, that I hoped it would not be an issue that I was gay. She nonchalantly told me that half the new staff was gay and it wouldn't be a concern. In the three years that I was there, only one virulently homophobic comment was made by a colleague—and it was rapidly addressed by the administration. The students and families all knew when I left the school that it was because my then-partner and I were adopting a child. They understood our desire to raise our son in a more racially diverse environment than Sonoma County and were genuinely sad to see me go.

When I accepted my last teaching job at an independent school in San Francisco, I did not even raise the issue of being gay. For one thing it was San Francisco, a gay mecca to legions of LGBT folks for generations, so I did not expect it to be a problem. Also, one of the science teachers at the school had worked with me at my first school, in Chicago, and my sense is that my résumé had been, in part, pulled out from a batch of equally qualified candidates. He was still partnered to the same person he had been with in Chicago. He was out then, and I assumed he was still out. So what did I have to fear?

But the feelings of discomfort about being a person of color lingered all those years and through those transitions. While my navigation of private schools as a gay teacher seemed relatively smooth, I cannot say this was the case for my navigation of the same spaces as a teacher of color. Race played out differently than sexual orientation in the conversations that I participated in and in the actions that I saw take place. At three of the four private schools I worked at I felt less safe identifying as an out teacher of color than I did identifying as an out LGBT teacher. The fourth school, the school in Sonoma County, was easily the place where I felt safest as a person of color. This was perhaps ironic because I was least involved in diversity programming around racial identity while I taught there, as compared to the other three schools.

The differences between moving through school spaces as a teacher of color and as an LGBT teacher were stark. As a teacher of color who advocated on behalf of students, teachers, and families of color, I felt like I was always navigating minefields. As an LGBT teacher, I did not feel this way. In three of the four schools, unlike my experience as a teacher of color, I never felt put on display as a gay person to represent an image the school tried to cultivate. I never had to fight entrenched interests to include LGBT issues in the curriculum because it could potentially upend "a classical education in humanities." When I supported LGBT issues I was never accused of being selfish or making issues of equity "about me." As an LGBT educator, I never felt like my value was the "flava'" that I brought because my family came from an exotic land. No one ever implied that, as a gay teacher, I was the diversity hire. When I spoke up about LGBT issues in a faculty meeting, no one from the majority group diminished the impact of what I had to say by feeling the need to state aloud that I was not speaking for everybody in my group. As an out LGBT educator I was never played off other LGBT educators and grouped into a "favored" or "unfavored" category based on how or what I was advocating. No older gay teacher ever took me aside and explained to me that I would have to work twice as hard to be considered just as good a teacher. And no one, when I talked about challenging moments LGBT teachers and LGBT students and families faced, threw their hands up in the air and said, "I don't think of you as gay. I just see you as a person. If we just don't talk about being gay, heterosexism will just go away!"

The difference between what many LGBT teachers experience and what their colleagues of color experience in independent schools has to do with the realities of independent schools' demographics. From what I saw, most independent schools were attended by large majority white (and fairly affluent) populations; the teaching staff, and in particular the leadership teams at independent schools (a number of teaching adults in such communities, like me, attended one themselves), often were less diverse than the populations they served. In my experience more than 90 percent of the teachers I worked with were white and 100 percent of administrators who were not admissions directors or directors of diversity were white.

But perhaps more important, those same people whom I worked with in the four schools I taught at had at least one gay person they were close to in their lives outside work. It might have been a close friend, a sibling, an in-law, or a relative. The same was not true when I considered how many of them had close friends of color outside work. (This anecdotal point is supported by a 2014 study conducted by the Public Religion Research Institute, which found that 75 percent of white Americans have no friends of color in their social networks.)

So, while many of them could understand the discrimination, both overt and structural, felt by many of their LGBT friends and loved ones, even some of the most liberal white colleagues I knew in these settings had no personal point of reference for understanding the existence and impact of White Privilege.

I will lean back into my earlier discussion of POCC for a minute to illustrate this. At some point, the POCC saw a rise in the number of white attendees participating in the conference. While this was a noble intention, it led to a good deal of hand wringing over whether the conference was about supporting people of color or having them educate people who were interested in helping them.

One of the hallmarks of the conference was its affinity-group structure. Unlike cultural appreciation groups, affinity groups are spaces where members share a specific identity and the focus is on group self-empowerment and support rather than the education of others. The affinity groups at the conference were organized by race. At perhaps the third or fourth POCC that I attended, a new affinity group was created for attendees who identified as LGBT, regardless of their race.

Curious, I went to the meeting.

It was a mixed group composed roughly equally of white educators and teachers of color. We sat in a large circle facing one another. The moderator was white and shared that he would be facilitating the discussion and taking notes. To his credit, he started with the provocative question of whether there needed to be an LGBT affinity group at the POCC. As I had been taught to do in my independent school education, I raised my hand and waited to be recognized. I looked around the room and saw other hands raised, mostly by the other LGBT teachers of color but also by some of the white teachers.

One of the white teachers in the group—without raising his hand or seemingly noticing that others had their hands raised—began to reply.

And then another did the same.

And then another. And another. And another.

The teachers of color continued to raise our hands and were recognized only when the white LGBT teachers had concluded.

No one—including the moderator—called them on this behavior. In a pattern I saw over and over again in the schools I worked in, White Privilege dominated the proceedings in a way heterosexual privilege did not. I'm sure a few of them, if they even noticed what happened, would not have been able to understand why the LGBT teachers of color had not said anything.

We were too busy worrying that if we were to do so, we would be characterized as aggressive, shrill, and confrontational—people who didn't understand that it wasn't *what* we were talking about that was problematic, it was *how* we were talking about it that made it hard for others to engage. It was hard to believe that this was happening at the People of Color Conference—a space created to empower people of color in independent schools. White Privilege fractured our supposed common ground as LGBT people.

But when I left teaching in independent schools, I left not because I was uncomfortable as a gay teacher—being an LGBT teacher in these types of schools was a relatively uncomplicated endeavor for me.

I left because I no longer wanted to be a teacher of color in that environment.

Interesting to me is that most of the LGBT colleagues I worked with as a teacher stayed in independent schools and, more often than not, stayed at the same school where I knew them. Conversely, more than half of the teachers of color I taught with are either no longer in independent schools or have moved on to another school.

Warren Reid at New England Minority Network (NEMNET), in presentations he gives about best practices for recruiting and retaining teachers of color, has pointed out that the average tenure for a teacher of color in independent schools is three years.

Three years.

I bear no ill will toward independent schools. I learned the craft of teaching in them, supported by resources and free of the classroom management realities that many of my colleagues in public schools have to contend with. I also know that in the independent schools I worked in, I built lasting professional and social networks and that I affected the lives of many students with whom I am still in contact today.

They were safe institutions to be an LGBT teacher.

But I don't know that I would ever go back to them as a teacher of color.

11

Many Strands, One Thread

Steven Benoit

FRENCH TEACHER
The Pingry School
Basking Ridge, New Jersey

This morning, sipping a mug of coffee in the cool June sunlight on Martha's Vineyard, I'm stopping for the first time in what feels like eons just to sit with my thoughts. Last weekend I both attended my sixteenth and final graduation at Solebury School and served as a pallbearer at my grandmother's funeral. I'm leaving the comfortable LGBT-friendly environment that I helped construct, and my staunchest ally and most vocal cheerleader has passed away. Without these two anchors, I'm feeling more than a little untethered.

Poised to trudge down a new path without those supports, I can't help but reflect on everything that led me to this moment. My coming-out journey and my evolution as a teacher started at roughly the same time, but the two trajectories are so different and—at least in the beginning—they were for two separate people: my work self and my real self. As I write today, I'm one man with many facets—an educator, a gay man, an advocate for LGBTQ youth, and a husband, among many others—but they're all part of one self. There's no need for reinvention, no professional veneer to don in the morning or shed at the end of the day. It's just me.

OUT OF THE CLOSET AND INTO THE CLASSROOM: AUSTIN, TEXAS
Rather than knock around the dusty hallways of my youth for too long, I'll start in Austin, where at age twenty-four, after moving across

the country, I landed in front of my first classroom at the University of Texas. The journey to that point was long and rough, even tragic at times. As a boy and young man, self-loathing to the brim, I wanted nothing more than to change my sexual orientation. I grew up in the 1970s and '80s, and there were exactly zero visible role models for gay youth at that time, no beacon to guide me through all that discomfort. The message I heard about homosexuality at home, church, and school and in the media was consistent: being gay was wrong, abhorrent, or, at best, funny. So I kept my secret locked tight, never speaking it aloud and never even writing about it in my private journal. If I didn't speak or write that simple clause "I'm gay," then maybe there was some sliver of hope that it wasn't true.

But at age twenty-four, I was ready to come out, to move toward something positive and constructive, and this needed to happen away from the people who knew me as straight. I accepted an offer to study French literature and teach undergraduate French at UT.

My first year in Austin was a hot, crazy mix of hard work and boundless fun. I dove into my graduate studies so deeply that it made my brain hurt. I made friends and enjoyed the hiking trails, the swimming holes, and the live music scene. After teaching my first classes, I knew immediately that I had stumbled into the right career. I had escaped my demons temporarily through a cocktail of academia, friendship, music, and the great outdoors.

In August 1993, as I entered the first class of my second year, chatting with a friend to my right, I sat down and glanced to my left. Something electric happened; I'll never forget the first time I laid my eyes on Mike. Those gorgeous blue-green eyes and that sweet smile took my breath away.

Mike and I chatted after class, and I learned that he had been living in Paris for my entire first year at UT. I was smitten but didn't have the slightest clue whether or not he was gay, and I dreaded treading down that hackneyed path of unrequited love for a straight man. We started spending hours together every day. We shared meals, studied, went swimming, worked out, hiked, played pool, bowled, and watched movies. As I look back, we were absolutely dating before we knew we were dating. It was the sweetest courtship I could have imagined, and it was exactly what I needed to tiptoe into the pool of relationships. A couple of months later, while camping with Mike in the Texas Hill Country, he touched my hand and asked if that would be okay, and trembling like crazy, I said yes. We kissed by the campfire, and with that kiss, my life changed forever.

We moved in together in December 1993, and everything about my life was almost surreal. Teaching was a blast; I was on track to finish my thesis not just on time but early; and I was sharing an apartment with a guy who'd shown me that I was indeed capable of falling deeply, irrevocably in love. Before this moment, I had never even dared entertain that possibility.

After a few months, I finally mustered the courage to come out to my immediate family. My mother was honest and open about her need for time to process. My older brother and my father closed the door on me completely, and that door has remained closed even to this day. My younger brother, then fourteen, reacted something like this: "Okay. Oh, hey, can you help me get Mom off my back about my grades?" For him, it was a nonissue.

The thought of telling my grandmother was terrifying, however. If my fourteen-year-old brother was the only immediate family member for whom my sexual orientation didn't matter, what chance did I stand with someone two generations away? All my life, Grandmom had held me up through tough times and cheered me on through victories. As my parents' marriage was crumbling, she kept me close and taught me to enjoy life even during the ugly moments. Later, she lent me the support I needed to become the first person from my family to attend college. My grandmother was my compass; losing her would hurt so much more deeply than the pain I felt when my father and older brother had turned their backs on me.

Within a week of those other family conversations, though, my grandmother called me. She cut to the chase: "Steve, your mother told me that you're gay. I will never stop loving you." Then she repeated:

"I will *never* stop loving you." I could hear the truth and warmth in her voice. From that moment forward, my grandmother would be my biggest ally for the next two decades.

TEACHING FROM THE CLOSET: NORTH CAROLINA

After our graduation from UT, master's degrees in hand, Mike and I moved to North Carolina. Mike had been accepted to the University of North Carolina's doctoral program, and I decided to take a leap of faith in our relationship. I flooded the Raleigh-Durham-Chapel Hill triangle with my résumé and fairly quickly heard from the head-mistress at a small school in Raleigh. When asked what was bringing me to North Carolina, I told a half-truth, saying that I had friends in Chapel Hill and that I was taking a break before pursuing my PhD. The position involved teaching French in their elementary school, but I'd be first in line if a spot opened up in their high school. We set up an interview for the day after our arrival in North Carolina. She offered me the job right then and there. Thus began chapter two of my teaching career.

That school was tough. Not metal-detector-in-the-hallway tough, but a delicately noxious environment for anyone nonstraight, non-Christian, nonwhite. The entire student body and faculty attended chapel a few times a week, and part of my charge was to teach the Lord's Prayer in French to all students in the school. I hadn't set foot in a church in years and here I was several times each week leading kids there and teaching them what to say. It left me off-kilter.

Compounding this, I quickly figured out that the bulk of the stake-holders at my new school worked in support of Senator Jesse Helms, whose most prominent legacy was bigotry—homophobia and rac-ism. I would be staying in the closet at work. Being an out employee there would not be tenable, and we needed my paltry paycheck.

Soon, a French position opened at the upper school. Teaching high school felt right, like kicking off my dress shoes and stepping into a comfy pair of slippers. Now I was excited to go to work. I could delve into the French language more deeply, and I connected with these students in ways I couldn't with the little ones. I saw my students every day, as opposed to once or twice weekly in the lower school, and they wanted to stay and talk after class. They were turning into adults before my eyes, and I felt lucky to be present for that metamorphosis. I'm not one of those people who always knew they wanted to teach high school; it just happened. Teaching in college was fun; teaching in elementary school could be a chore; teaching in high school was *home.*

It wasn't long before I started feeling like a fraud there as well, though. There were a couple of students who I was pretty sure were gay, and I just wanted to reach out and tell them that they weren't alone, that they'd be okay. However, I still couldn't risk being out.

The following year, the school added a sex education program for students. Everyone piled into the chapel (yes, the chapel), and a few students' moms (yes, moms) came in to deliver the "curriculum." Their message was that when a young man and young woman developed feelings for each other, they needed to deny the physical urges until they were older and in a position to get married. They told the students that they would be hearing things about condoms and safe sex, but that they'd never need condoms, because they'd only ever have sex with their spouse; that sex was only to happen between one man and one woman in the context of sacred matrimony. *That* was the only safe sex.

And then came the blinding-white rage. I could say with certainty that these two women were passing out death warrants to some of those students, gay or straight, male or female. They were kicking all the LGBTQ kids to the back of the closet and locking the door with a deadbolt, then pushing a dresser in front of the door, and then maybe setting the whole house on fire for good measure. This message was hurtful, dangerous.

Mike and I decided that we would leave the South at the end of that school year, so I got bolder in small ways. We quietly exchanged rings and registered as domestic partners in Carrboro, North Carolina, which carried no legal benefits but felt symbolically huge. This was a matter of public record, so it could have led to my being fired. I affixed a bumper sticker to my car: "I live in North Carolina and I do not support Jesse Helms." I put a Darwin fish plaque right beside that sticker. One day after school, I noticed that someone had ripped off the Darwin fish. I bought another plaque on my way home that night, so it was on my car the very next morning at work. The thief left that one alone, resigned to my tenacity.

As Mike was finishing his doctoral dissertation, we began our search for two French-teaching jobs within commuting distance of each other—but only in the Northeast or along the Pacific coast. I decided to be out and open in my interviews. This was in the winter of 1997–98, and hiring and firing based on sexual orientation was still legal in most states (as it still is in twenty-nine states as of 2014). I decided that if I couldn't find a teaching job as an out gay man, although it'd make me sad, I'd forge a different career path. My own mental health had to come first. A battering ram was in order for that closet door.

That February I was invited to Solebury School in New Hope, Pennsylvania. I drove up for an interview and stayed with my grandmother, who lived about an hour from the school. She was over the moon at the prospect of having me nearby again. It was my first interview, and boy was Solebury different from my current employer. Students addressed teachers by their first name. The diversity in the student body was palpable, visible. The school had no religious affiliation, and anarchy of many kinds seemed to prevail. I fell in love with Solebury.

I made good on my resolve to be out in the interview, explaining that both Mike and I were looking for jobs together. No one balked at that until the Residential Life folks broached the topic of on-campus housing. When I mentioned that Mike and I shared a home, they made it clear that this would not be possible on campus. Today, I'd be outraged by such a proclamation, but back then I was just overjoyed that they were even considering me for the position. At the end of my eight-hour interview, as I trudged against the icy wind to my car, three students I'd met that day intercepted me and wished me luck, saying that they thought I'd be a great fit. I thanked them and shook their hands, all the while thinking, "Where am I? In what universe do students feel so comfortable approaching strange adults and talking like this?"

The director of studies (a position I'd occupy myself about fourteen years later) called me within a few days and offered me the post. Given the dense concentration of independent schools in the Pennsylvania–New Jersey area, Mike and I decided that I should accept the offer and we'd flood the region with his résumé. Mike eventually received an offer from a school in northern New Jersey, and we started making our plans to move.

COMING HOME

In June of 1998 we packed a U-Haul and the car we shared, left Dixie, and headed north. Later that same school year, thanks to a little help from my grandmother, Mike and I would buy our first house together.

Being an out-and-proud teacher at Solebury School has been a process, not an event, just like it is for LGBTQ folks everywhere in the world. Since day one on campus I've been living my life honestly and unapologetically. I felt compelled to debunk the gay lifestyle myth for the people with whom I worked. Once when a new teacher, upon hearing that I lived with another teacher, asked me what my wife taught, I responded with a smile and said, "My *husband* also teaches French." The teacher's eyes widened for a moment, and my colleagues within earshot grinned, but that was the extent of the reaction.

A steady trickle of students started coming out to me, tentatively and slowly. The first was an eighth grader. He entered my classroom before school one day; if he'd been a dog, his tail would have hung between his legs. I looked up from my lesson plans and greeted him with a hearty "Bonjour." After a pregnant pause, he asked if it would freak me out if he told me he was gay. I said, "Of course not. I'm gay too." He actually had known about me; I'd regularly refer to my partner when talking to students, but this young man had never heard me utter those explicit words. That day, this student opened up about his hopes and fears about coming out, and we talked about the implications of being open with family and friends. That conversation left me fulfilled in a completely new way.

From that moment forward, every time a student would come out to me, my ability to be present and honest felt like a living amends to the students in Raleigh with whom I couldn't be honest, the ones who were forced to endure the mom-chapel-sex-education talk. Somewhere along the way, I had become a quiet, almost accidental activist, and the role fit like a glove. I worked with a few friends to start a Gay-Straight Alliance, which we called Spectrum, and which soon became one of the most active clubs on campus.

At that time I was the only out member of the faculty, and that could be a lonely spot. In 2002, when I went to a diversity conference sponsored by the National Association of Independent Schools, I attended their affinity group for LGBTQ teachers. Around the room, a chorus of teachers voiced the same issues I'd been facing: "I'm afraid people will think I'm recruiting," and "So many view gay people as pedophiles, and what if people accuse me of things if I come out?" The strength I drew from that gathering blew me away.

One day later that school year, a student came to Spectrum, visibly upset, talking about some graffiti in a men's bathroom on campus that read "Die fags!" The school's reaction went from shock ("Even here?") to outrage. A brief faculty meeting had already been scheduled for that morning and a few of us brought up this issue there, ready to rally teachers into action. One colleague made a suggestion: at the next assembly, she'd make an announcement about the incident, and then other teachers and administrators would stand up behind her to denounce the vandalism and its message. What I hadn't expected was the resistance that came. One teacher actually said, "I don't want students to think I believe that it's okay to be gay." The assembly idea was nixed; the graffiti was painted over, and no other action was taken. That protest and subsequent inaction hurt deeply, and for a few weeks I couldn't even bring myself to eat lunch in the dining hall. I just kept to myself and focused purely on my work with students.

Within a couple of years, I finally had some out company on campus. We had an influx of LGBTQ teachers—more than 10 percent of our faculty at one point. One social studies candidate, an out lesbian, accepted the position largely because of our work with diversity, and she quickly became my right arm in Spectrum. She and I even launched a summer conference for LGBTQ teachers in 2011, a successful endeavor that I soon had to leave by the wayside when I accepted the position of director of studies.

As a full-time administrator, many different challenges came across my desk: boredom was not part of my lexicon. However, I missed my time with the *students* at school. I was still teaching one class, kept my commitment with Spectrum, and had a slate of advisees. To a nonteacher, that might sound like a lot of face time with teenagers, but it wasn't enough for me. I was feeling disconnected from my teaching roots.

Those contacts with students provided the charge to my professional batteries. I thought back to some young folks who had affected me deeply along the way. There was a young woman, "Chantal," whom I'd taught for four years in a row. We had a wonderful rapport and she was a star student in all the classes she took with me, but somehow her bubble at school had prevented her from learning that I was gay. One day when we were around the table at a diversity meeting, I alluded to my sexual orientation. You could watch the cartoonish impact on her face; imagine an anvil to Wile E. Coyote. After that meeting she avoided me. In class she wouldn't make eye contact or speak, except to answer content-specific questions, and there was no more of that before- or after-class banter that I'd come to expect and cherish.

After the end of one class, I asked her to stay, and once the other students had left, I asked her, "Did learning that I'm gay freak you out?" She answered honestly that, yes, it had. "I've never known anyone gay before. I'm from a very religious family," she said. I gently pointed out that of course she'd known gay people before; it's just that she hadn't known that they were gay. I also shared that I knew plenty of religious gay people. I told her that I hoped this wouldn't change our rapport, because she was one of my favorite people. And it wasn't long before things were back to normal. Chantal came early and stuck around after class just to chat. As she graduated, she asked her parents to take a photo of us. We're friends now on Facebook, many years later.

Another former student (whom I'll call Katz) jumps to mind—a gifted musician, a scholar, an athlete, and a deep thinker. As fate would have it, his parents needed help getting him to school, and they lived roughly on my path between home and work. He became my copilot for four years. He started attending Spectrum; I continued teaching French to him; we chatted for hours every week on our commute. He eventually became the student president of Spectrum, and occasionally he'd mention, "So-and-so doesn't believe that I'm straight because of all the work I do in Spectrum." His tone was more amused and bemused than frustrated. He was and is a passionate advocate for equality around LGBTQ issues.

Katz evolved into much more than a student for me; he became family. Every senior gets his or her own page in the yearbook, for photos and shout-outs. On Katz's senior page, he called me "My best friend, my buddy, my second father." He continues to be part of my life, calling or writing with news both good and bad. When he comes back to town, we meet for lunch or dinner. He's like the son I never had.

Last year, 2013, the tide began to turn on marriage equality as the US Supreme Court overturned the Defense of Marriage Act. When New Jersey's decision on the issue was pending last fall, all members of Spectrum were on the edge of their seats. I mentioned that, if the news was positive, I would be getting married right away. I explained the impeccable timing—that Mike and I were about to celebrate our twentieth anniversary, and that these two events might even coincide.

I'd never heard such a cheer erupt from a classroom, and word spread like wildfire across campus. A young sophomore made me a congratulations card, signed by almost the entire student body. The New Jersey Supreme Court handed down their decision (yes!), and Mike and I were able to apply for our marriage license the day before our anniversary, though we had to wait seventy-two hours before getting married. We went out to a romantic anniversary dinner, extra sweet because of the impending wedding, at a gorgeous inn on the

Delaware River. At the end of the meal when we asked for the check, the concierge told us that my boss had taken care of the bill, and that he hadn't been the only one to try to do that. He told us that he'd never seen anything like it, and he congratulated us on our two decades together. All that week we were inundated with flowers, cards, and well wishes. Solebury School was cheering for us, quite literally.

Mike and I were legally married twenty years and two days after that camping trip in the Texas Hill Country where we pledged our love for each other. It was to be in a simple ceremony. However, some of Mike's and my favorite colleagues appeared with balloons and streamers; they told us that there was no way they were going to miss this momentous occasion. Not long after all this, I received a message from a friend in another school, asking me to consider applying for an opening there. I said, "No thanks," but then, given my ambivalence about my administrative position, I opted to go and see what the place was like. They ended up making me an offer as a full-time French teacher, with a few other responsibilities. The more I thought about this, the more intrigued I became at the prospect of diving back into the classroom, in a day school that was much closer to home. After many conversations with a handful of colleagues at Solebury, after much exhortation from Mike (how could I not respond to his sweet "I miss my husband!" pleas?), and after many hours of soul searching, I accepted the position.

I don't know which was harder—breaking the news to the people I cared deeply about or the actual good-byes. There were many tears—both expected and unexpected—from students and colleagues and myself. One of the sweetest moments came when Spectrum threw a good-bye party; they presented me with a collection of Mary Oliver poems, signed by all the members.

In the midst of bidding farewell to Solebury, I was also in the process of saying good-bye to my grandmother. During my last week of classes, she was diagnosed with cancer, and I made the two-hour trek to be by her side a few times a week. She could no longer speak, but she was alert; she would hold my hand and listen to the stories I'd tell her. Grandmom passed away a mere ten days after her diagnosis.

I can't stop (and hope I never do) thinking about my grandmother, this powerhouse, this wonderful human being whose love and support never wavered. Even in the last couple of years of her life, as dementia began to steal her memories, she remained full of love and joy. During the final months of her life when I'd arrive to visit, her face would light up, and she'd tell me that she must be dreaming, that she was so happy to see me. Then she'd admit that she didn't know who I was. I'd remind her, "I'm Steve, your grandson," and I'd point to the photo on her shelf, the one of Mike and me hiking on the Oregon coast. Each time, she'd say, "Oh, but that's the gay one. Are you gay?" I'd assure her that I was. And without fail, *every time*, she'd respond, "Oh, that doesn't matter. I love you no matter what. I'll always love you."

And she did.

Now here I sit, within earshot of the ocean on the Vineyard, only one week after the funeral-graduation weekend. I'm spending this week gathering my thoughts, to digest, to process. It's hard to imagine what next week will be like when we're back in New Jersey.

I don't know much more than this: I'll be fine—better than fine— outside my comfort zone for a while. The strength I've drawn from my grandmother and from my time at Solebury won't just evaporate; I'll carry that with me wherever I go. Come August in my new school, I'll be unapologetically and uneventfully out and proud to my new students and colleagues. I'll savor being back in the classroom with students all day.

As I look at who I am today, I can scarcely connect the dots to the fearful, self-loathing teenager I once was. These days, being gay for me is no different than my eye color, my skin color, or my height. It's just part of the fabric that makes me who I am. Those different strands of my identity have all woven together into one thread; it's a privilege, an honor, to bring my whole, complex self into the classroom.

12

Coming Out at Fifty

Garth Zimmermann

RETIRED TEACHER
Appleton, Wisconsin, Area School District
Appleton, Wisconsin

"I have never told any student this for thirty-seven years. I am gay, happy, and proud of who I am. My only sin against God is not accepting the person he made me to be for so long. Anyone who because of their religion harasses someone for being gay better not have eaten any shrimp, because according to Leviticus, they're headed to the same place they say I am. Know that people support you, love you, and have your back."

I was speaking to two sixth-grade boys sitting across the table from me in my classroom. One of the young men, Danny, had been the recipient of a female student's harassment outside school. Her family belonged to a Bible-based megachurch just blocks from our school, and she told Danny he was sinful for being gay and he was "going to hell" because of it. The young man had become emotionally exhausted and was becoming withdrawn both inside and outside the classroom. His friend Doug, who was sitting next to him as I spoke, was there to support Danny. He was a young man I knew I could trust. Doug's older brother knew I was gay, and I was correct that he knew as well. As they left, you could see the burden lift from Danny's shoulders, and he became a frequent visitor to my classroom before school.

Shortly afterward, I began reflecting on my own journey through life and teaching that had led me to this moment.

I grew up in central Wisconsin, home to many dairy farms like the one my parents owned and purchased from my grandparents. I was the youngest child, the only boy, with two sisters who were thirteen and seventeen years older than I. My mother always commented that she had a high school graduation, confirmation, and baptism all in the same year. By the time I was six, both of my sisters had married and I became the only child in our household. I knew my parents loved each other, with my mom joining my dad in the barn every morning at five to milk cattle and perform other chores before coming into the house to make breakfast. My mom joked in her later years that she maintained her health by being a "strong farm woman," baling and unloading hay, running farm machinery, feeding and cleaning up after cattle. On a dairy farm, the work is constant, and my father always managed to come up with a to-do list every morning. Neither of my parents graduated from high school, my dad going to a one-room schoolhouse until he "graduated" in eighth grade, my mom dropping out of Green Bay East High School as a junior to help her mother raise her twin grandsons when *their* mother died of tuberculosis. This lack of schooling didn't prevent my parents from successfully operating a dairy farm nor was it an obstacle to their respecting both education and educators.

The most powerful social organization within our rural community was Zion Lutheran Church, a tall, wood-sided white building with a proud steeple and no indoor bathrooms. We were Missouri Synod Lutherans, but it wasn't until years later that I realized the active social conservatism within the church. Every Sunday we would go to church, listening to our minister explain Bible passages and parables. My mom was a member of the Ladies Aid, my dad an usher and member of the Men's Club that met regularly. I went to Sunday School for eight years, was confirmed after attending two years of Saturday morning confirmation classes (which got me out of farm chores), read scripture from the pulpit with a voice that everyone could easily hear, ushered each week, and in eighth grade even entertained the idea of becoming a minister.

No one spoke of sex, much less sexual orientation, much less same-sex sexual orientation, in our community. Growing up, I never heard the words *homosexual, gay,* or *lesbian.* But in high school I knew something was different about me, and not just the fact that, except for a few close friends, I tended to be an outsider. I wasn't attracted to girls like other guys were, and I found myself admiring the bodies of individual male athletes in school or carnival workers at our fair. I still had no clue what any of this meant, even as I entered college.

Because of my positive experiences as a 4-H Junior Leader, I decided to major in elementary education at University of Wisconsin–Stevens Point. I loved teaching and somehow knew I had the organizational and communication skills to be successful in the classroom. At this time I was also beginning to recognize my sexual orientation through reading books like *The Lord Won't Mind,* which I secretly looked at in the campus library, or watching an episode of *All in the Family,* which featured Archie finding out his football-playing buddy was gay. Still, I repressed my feelings and never acted upon them. I would meet the expectations of both my church and society to get married, raise a family, and "control" any feelings of attraction I had toward men. In college I met Judy, and we began a courtship that lasted seven years until we were married.

My first full-time teaching position took me to Birchwood, a K–12 school of 270 students in northwestern Wisconsin. This was the fall of 1977, and I was excited to have a job teaching middle school science and reading, and I also took on the position of coaching girls junior varsity basketball. It was after my switch to coach boys varsity basketball in 1981 that the rumors began about my sexuality. I had replaced a prominent parent as coach, thus becoming unpopular on day one. I was criticized for a variety of reasons, but my most vivid memory is when a colleague told me people thought I was too negative with players. Sarcastically I replied, "What should I do? Kiss a player when he leaves the court?" His eyes grew wide, and he quickly and emphatically responded, "Oh my God, don't do that." Right then I knew what the community was saying behind my back, that I was probably gay and had no business coaching boys. While the rumors and innuendo bothered me, I had just married and hoped that would put any allegations to rest. I was fired from the position two years later. In hindsight, I believe perceptions about my sexual orientation became an underlying—and unspoken—reason for my dismissal.

In 1985 we moved back to central Wisconsin when I accepted a sixth-grade teaching position in the Wittenberg-Birnamwood School District, along with the position of middle school boys basketball coach. One year later my wife and I had our first of three children. I was Teacher of the Year in my first year and loved teaching students in a rural district whose backgrounds were similar to mine. Over the next seven years I was a highly successful teacher and coach, father, and yes, husband. My attraction to men remained, no matter how much I tried to change my thinking while remaining faithful to our marriage. Even in the 1980s, except for an adult bookstore in nearby Wausau, gay wasn't anywhere to be seen, much less discussed.

Appleton, Wisconsin, is a city of about seventy-one thousand people thirty minutes south of "the Frozen Tundra" of Lambeau Field, where our beloved Green Bay Packers play. In 1992 I was pleased to accept a position at Wilson Middle School in Appleton, a district with a statewide reputation for excellence and innovation. During that time I received a Kohl Fellowship for teaching excellence. Professionally, I was at the top of my career.

During that same time, however, my personal life was falling apart. After successful bariatric weight loss surgery in which Judy lost more than one hundred pounds, she found a new addiction: alcohol. The day before 9/11 she was picked up for OWI (operating while intoxicated) in Fond Du Lac while searching for my son's freshman football game. The second OWI came two weeks later, when she was driving down an interstate highway in the wrong direction. Her first inpatient treatment was at Hazelden that January. Following a relapse several months later and while in her second inpatient facility, we separated, eventually divorcing in 2003 because of her repeated relapses into alcoholism. I blamed myself for her alcoholism and deep down probably hoped the divorce would bring her the physical and emotional happiness she lacked throughout her lifetime. That fall, sitting alone in a hotel whirlpool, I reflected on my life. At forty-eight years of age, I finally accepted the idea of coming out if the rest of my life was to be open, happy, and honest.

Our school district had an EAP (employee assistance program), and I found an amazing counselor who helped me cope with Judy's alcoholism. Coming out to her in her office was a whole different situation. My nerves were in high gear. I said the words "I'm gay." Her response: "So?" My next words let out my guilt: "Which caused my wife to be an alcoholic." She then looked me straight in the eye and said, "I've met a lot of women whose husbands are gay, and none of them is an alcoholic." My coming out had begun.

By November 2005 I had come out to my kids, close friends, and my then eighty-five-year-old mother, who embraced me with her love. Through a local coffeehouse, I met a support and social group for gays and lesbians. I was ready to come out to Judy, but two days after Thanksgiving, she was found dead at her home, the cause being cirrhosis of the liver. The years that followed were difficult, be it from my still working through guilt and eventually acceptance or being a single father whose teenage kids had dealt with alcoholism, coming out, divorce, and now the death of a parent over the course of several years. I had realized the personal costs and consequences of being in the closet and now wanted to help others with accepting themselves and achieving their full potential.

The real turning point came when I attended the NEA (National Education Association) Representative Assembly in Washington, DC, in 2008. There I met other LGBT educators from across the country in an LGBT caucus and attended a dinner of celebration and recognition of LGBT educators. Inspired, I came home to Appleton and met with Hank, the WEAC (Wisconsin Education Association Council)—Fox

Valley unit director, who in turn drove me to Madison to meet with and have my questions and concerns answered by a WEAC lawyer. One week later, with my local union president in attendance, I came out in a meeting with my district superintendent and an assistant superintendent, and was assured that there was not a problem. I remember asking one question in particular: "What if a conservative parent objects to having me teach his or her child because I'm gay?" The response: "We have open enrollment in our district, and they could choose to drive their student to a different school." My fears were unfounded. I came out and found acceptance from both my administration and my fellow staff members.

I served as the NEA-GLBT Midwest Caucus director for four years and as a gay representative on the WEAC Human Relations Committee. Even though I never mentioned it openly, it didn't take long for my students to figure out I was gay. By accepting myself, I reached my full potential both inside and outside the classroom. The guilt of living a lie was gone, the fear of being found out removed, and I was both joyous and grateful to have a second chance to live an honest, open life and let people know the true me. Then, thanks to Match.com, I met an amazing man who has become my life partner.

Two years ago, with the assistance of our city diversity coordinator, I developed a forty-minute LGBT lesson to be used as part of our sixth-grade human growth and development curriculum at Houdini Elementary School, where I have taught since 2004. The focus is on what LGBT means and includes examples of famous individuals from all areas of life who are LGBT, an antibullying role play, and, finally, an It Gets Better Project video featuring Google employees. Twenty-five sets of parents attended the preview night for the unit: to say that I was nervous, even after thirty-five years of teaching, was an understatement. My building principal and two teaching colleagues were there to offer support. Once again, my fears were unfounded. The lesson was accepted by parents, who used the opportunity to open discussions with their sons and daughters. I have been impressed by the high interest level of students and how well they role-play responses to a bullying scenario within the lesson. I was observed teaching the lesson by my building principal, our guidance counselor, and our district curriculum coordinator, each one praising and complimenting both the content and the presentation.

Even in retirement, my passion that every LGBT student accepts and celebrates who he or she is will continue. I recognize there are many pathways on which this passion may take me in the future. For Danny, I can only hope the teacher I have become will help him become a man whose life reaches its full potential.

13

Finding a Way and Making One: Coming Out Brown, Feminist, and Queer

Ileana Jiménez

ENGLISH TEACHER
Little Red School House and Elisabeth Irwin High School (LREI)
New York, New York

Then one day, I was called into the head of school's office.

I knew what was coming. The new issue of the school newspaper had just been released. I had been the advisor since my arrival in 1999, when I was a twenty-four-year-old blazing feminist and was known to approve of stories and op-eds that critiqued the school's conservative values.

I was also known to be a stickler for strong writing and balanced reporting. I had won the University of Maryland's young newspaper advisor award. During my tenure, the paper also won awards from the prestigious Columbia Scholastic Press Association, and I had been invited to be a judge for their annual competition.

One year, the girls wanted to do a special section on diversity, or the lack thereof, at their elite girls' school just outside Washington, DC. They wanted to do a piece about the lack of writers of color in the English program, another about spending a semester away and meeting queer kids for the first time, and another featuring the one out lesbian science teacher.

I told the girls that it was a great idea. To make sure we had a balanced issue, I advised them to do a special pullout section on the construction happening on campus. With a multimillion dollar project involving a new art studio, black box theater, a lecture hall, science labs, and a track and field, the school was poised to reveal its shiny gems in just a few months.

Within days after the new issue release, the head of school wrote me an e-mail saying she wanted to meet. I knew what was up. I knew she didn't want to talk about the great photos of yellow tractors and construction workers.

I immediately did my homework on the First Amendment, which does not protect private school students. Even so, the websites I researched suggested, what school would want to deny students basic rights already granted to them in a democracy? I wrote down my talking points.

When I entered her office, she was sitting at her desk near a large bay window that gave her a full view of the school's green grounds. Hers was one of the few offices that were carpeted and I treaded lightly on the plush blue. Another white and ruby Oriental carpet marked off a small sitting area. She motioned me to sit on the flowered sofa.

While I waited for her to finish at her desk, I looked around. A coffee table in front of me held the school's publications, including the new issue of the newspaper. I stared at its front page as if asking for strength. The school's motto was emblazoned on the masthead: "*Inveniam viam aut faciam*" (I will find a way or make one).

"Thank you for coming," she said, seating herself on a Chippendale chair. "I wanted to speak to you about the paper."

I will find a way or make one, I thought.

"There's an article involving Ginny. Does she know about it?" she looked at me with her purple and gray eyes.

"Yes, she gave us permission," I said.

"I'm glad. We are a K–12 institution. It's not appropriate for us to cover certain issues given the range of ages here."

"Which issues are you referring to?" I asked.

"We've had some calls from parents about the piece on sexuality."

There it was. At least she said it. The fear of parents in many schools is what keeps so many teachers and administrators on the straight and narrow—literally and metaphorically. Even so, I was irritated but not surprised that she hadn't the courage to defend our students' rights.

I reminded her that there were not one but two pieces that touched on sexual identity. There was one about a senior girl who had gone to Colorado for a semester, where she happened to meet some great queer kids who became her friends. The other was about Ginny, the one out teacher at the school, and the importance of having Gay-Straight Alliances.

Then I said, "The girls wanted to write about diversity. We believe in encouraging them to find their voices. It's in the mission statement."

Her steel-gray eyes widened. "We have lots of publications here, and the school newspaper is one of them, and we need to be responsible about what we publish."

"We are responsible," I said. "By school publications you must mean those that come out of the advancement office that are made by adults. Other than the literary magazine and the yearbook, which only come out once a year, this is the one publication whose content is regularly created by the students. The upper school girls can't be censoring their articles just because a kindergarten student might read it."

Her eyes iced over. "The parents have concerns."

"If I were the head," I said looking into her eyes, "I would've reminded those parents about our mission. They've committed to providing their daughters with every opportunity. The girls are doing the very thing we are teaching them to do."

Her eyes clouded.

I had found a way, but barely.

When I was hired by not one but two girls' schools within two years of graduating from college, I thought I was going to live out my dream.

I had gone to Smith, a women's college, and it changed my life. As a first generation student whose parents had never received a higher education, my going to Smith vindicated all the hardworking years my Puerto Rican parents had put into raising us, first in the Bronx and then later on Long Island.

My father had grown up on a tobacco farm in a large family of sharecroppers in Puerto Rico, and my mother had grown up first on the island and then later in the Bronx. My father served in the army and later became an NYPD cop. My mom attended Morris High School, where she had been discouraged from going on to college. Told by her guidance counselor that she should go to vocational school instead, my mother became one of the founding secretaries in the first Puerto Rican studies departments at both Lehman and John Jay Colleges in New York. After years of service, my parents wanted one thing for us: a higher education that would give us a better life than they had.

My time at Smith was a women-only wonderland of feminist academia and politics. Sexual politics, in particular. It was the height of the gay nineties, and Smith was living those years up in their classic women-rule-the-world style. I was surrounded by lesbian professors and lesbian friends all day long and loved it.

Even before coming to Smith, I'd had my feminist epiphany in high school. But Smith's culture solidified my instincts and gave me the language to express what I had felt all along: that I was a Puerto Rican feminist lesbian with a pipe dream of becoming a teacher.

On top of that, Smith converted me into a single-sex education believer. As an English major, I would dream about teaching in girls' schools. I had this fantasy that girls' schools were just like Smith, full of awesome feminist faculty, feminist students, and feminist books. While studying Shakespeare and Milton, Austen and Woolf in Seelye Hall, I would envision myself teaching the very books I was reading and annotating. I would listen to my professors lecture while designing elaborate curriculum plans in the margins of my notebooks.

I wanted to teach young women the same books that led me to me. Reading feminist books in high school and then later in college allowed me to find myself. I wanted young women to have that same opportunity for self-discovery. For that reason, I wanted to teach them books that I had read not only in my literature courses but also in my women's studies classes. I was in love with the idea of exposing young women to Chicana feminist writers like Cherríe Moraga and Gloria Anzaldúa and black feminist writers like Audre Lorde and bell hooks.

Ultimately, I wanted to give young women what Smith had given me: a feminist education and a feminist identity.

The gold insignia of College Hall on my school notebooks might as well have been tattooed on my skin if not my heart. If Smith could transform this Puerto Rican girl from the Bronx into an inspired feminist teacher, then I would turn legions of girls and young women into feminists too.

But girls' schools are not women's colleges.

Quite the opposite.

My early teaching days in two different girls' schools—first in Baltimore and then outside Washington—were a young feminist's nightmare. I learned quickly that teachers and administrators in single-sex schools had learned a different definition of feminism than I had learned at Smith.

They wanted to teach power feminism.

I wanted to teach social justice feminism.

Their version of feminism was about parading illustrious alums and other wealthy women leaders in front of the girls as "inspiration" for future corporate careers and status quo lives.

I wanted to teach the girls to be radical, which I equated with Angela Davis's definition: "Radical simply means 'grasping things at the root.'"

And, as Toni Morrison writes in her Nobel Prize lecture, "narrative is radical," so I taught my students to write radical stories about themselves.

Of course I taught them how to write eloquent five-paragraph essays about *The Great Gatsby*, but I also wanted them to tell their own truths. There were so many other assignments these girls had to complete that kept them suffocated in a school that squeezed them into plaid uniforms that were meant for children and into boxes that were meant for objects.

In my classes, all silences were broken. The wealthy white girls wrote stories about being white and privileged. Girls of color from all socioeconomic backgrounds wrote about wanting to confront the racism and classism at school. The queer girls wrote about wanting to come out. The Asian girls wrote about being invisible. The dancer girls wrote about being forced to become anorexic or bulimic at their Washington, DC, dance schools. And because of the time period, the Muslim girls wrote about being afraid to be seen as September 11 terrorists.

All of them thanked me for giving them the chance to write themselves into existence.

The girls quickly caught on to what type of teacher I was.

One day, two girls, one white and one Indian, approached me.

"Ms. Jiménez, we want you to be our GSA advisor!" they squealed.

I felt my stomach drop. I was both honored and horrified. I was not out at the school. Did these girls know I was gay? Could they see through me? A rush of scenes from the English classes I taught them ran through my head as I tried to find the moment when they might've guessed the truth.

My mind stopped to a scene earlier that fall when I had shared some articles about women and queer people that I had collected from the *Washington Post*. I had used these articles as a springboard for the girls to brainstorm possible research paper topics. The school was celebrating their centennial and I thought it would be great to mark the event by encouraging—not requiring—my students to consider doing a paper on any national or global women's issue. It was a girls' school, after all.

Instead, I received a lengthy e-mail from one father who excoriated me for standing on my "feminist soapbox." He finished the e-mail by saying he didn't want me to "brainwash" his daughter with all this feminist trash.

I was flabbergasted that a parent who sent his daughter to a girls' school would complain that his daughter was being taught about girls and women. This e-mail was swiftly followed up with a meeting behind closed doors with my English department chair. She took care of the situation, but I was far from off the hook. For the entire five years I spent at the school, I felt like I was being watched.

As the girls excitedly jumped around me in their green-and-blue-plaid uniform skirts, I realized that I could not lead the school's first Gay-Straight Alliance without being seen as the instigator, even though it was their idea.

I looked into their eyes and knew they were in that critical phase of exploring their sexual identity. I had watched them in the hallways and heard their conversations. Queer kids don't necessarily talk about being queer, but they do talk about things that other kids don't. Some queer kids love art and film and music and theater. Others talk politics and policy. Most have a deep understanding of outsiderness and feel protective of others in pain, even if they don't yet know that it's their own they're protecting.

These girls were asking me because they needed me, and whether or not they knew I was queer was not the point. Given all my assignments and all my closeted talk of being an ally, they knew I was a teacher they could trust.

I couldn't let them down. I had to think of something that both affirmed their choice in me and yet protected me from further scrutiny. I was closeted yet political. I was a proud young feminist and yet a scared femme dyke. I was living a double life of empowering young women when they were in front of me and cowering behind my desk when they left the classroom. I was encouraging them to be independent and self-actualized and yet I could not model what a fully self-actualized woman was like.

On top of that, I was one of only a few teachers of color at the school, and of those few, I was the only one who made my Latina teacher identity a political one. I attended conferences for teachers of color and presented on my feminist work in the classroom. I spoke out at faculty meetings and, although I'm not proud of it, had once made an administrator—who happened to be a closeted lesbian—cry.

I realize now that my constant speaking out was my way of coming out. The closet could not completely hold me in. And yet, given my reputation, I couldn't risk being seen as both an outspoken woman of color and an outspoken lesbian. I was already marked.

More important, I feared being rejected by the girls of color who saw me as one of their own in a school that was elite white and elite privileged. I was afraid of coming out too soon and losing the solidarity I had built with the black and Latina girls. I foolishly thought that being seen as straight by these girls would sustain their acceptance of me. What I didn't realize was that there could've been queer girls of color who needed me too. Indeed, standing right in front of me was a young Indian girl pleading with me to found the school's first GSA.

I had to say yes, but on my own terms.

"I can be your GSA advisor if you get at least one other teacher to do it along with me. I'm also the advisor to the newspaper and I can't do two clubs by myself," I said in one breath.

"Yes, okay! Let's ask Ms. Whittier!" they said in unison.

I agreed that asking the school psychologist was a sound choice, even though she had once introduced me to a student as Ms. Rodriguez and glazed over the mistake by saying that all Latino names sounded the same. When I had approached her about it privately, she apologized and said she didn't realize she had been so insensitive.

As I said yes to my new GSA girls, I crossed my fingers hoping that Ms. Whittier would not demonstrate any lazy homophobia in the same way that she had shown her lazy racism.

Most important, I thought, was that Ms. Whittier was respected by the administration, she was white, and she was straight.

I organized our first GSA event by reaching out to a major national LGBT rights group in Washington. They led me to members of their advisory board who were interested in speaking to young people.

While on the phone with Laura, who was white, and Radha, who was Indian, Radha said something that shot me straight back to my women's studies days at Smith.

"I want to share with young women what it means to be brown and lesbian," she declared.

I looked over at my copy of Cherríe Moraga's *Loving in the War Years*, a book I'd discovered while taking a Latina women writers class in college. Between its covers was an essay that had broken open my identity when I was just nineteen years old. Moraga wrote, "My brother's sex was white. Mine, brown."

I wanted to cry through the phone, "I'm brown and lesbian too!" but I held my tongue. I just continued to act like a goody-goody ally who was happily booking two lesbian speakers for her school.

When I introduced Laura and Radha during the assembly, I looked over at the closeted administrator I had made cry earlier that year. Had she cried because she was tired of the charade too? Was she glad that I was doing something she didn't have the guts to do? Should I just out the both of us right here, right now while on stage?

Or should I just out myself in front of the whole school?

I introduced Laura and Radha instead. Radha turned out to be a femme dyke of color just like me. She wore makeup, heels, and a flattering corporate outfit that had all the girls doubting she was queer. I remember feeling envious that she was so out and proud and femme and brown.

I wondered, where had my Smith self gone? What had happened to me in just a few short years after graduating?

As I sat there listening to Laura and Radha share their life stories, I was desperate to climb up on stage and proclaim: "I, your young upstart teacher from Smith, the one who teaches you *The Scarlet Letter*, am a brown lesbian."

I was Hester Prynne, except my burning letter was hidden underneath my red Ann Taylor sweater.

One day I was tired of it all and just left.

I was tired of being brought into back rooms. Tired of being told I was too radical. Too political. Too feminist. Too me.

I was tired of being watched.

So I left.

I had three goals in mind. I was twenty-nine years old and promised myself that before I turned thirty, I would come out to my family, come out professionally, and find a school that would allow me to be a wholly queer and feminist teacher.

That spring of 2004, I left the world of conservative girls' schools and the conservative politics of Washington and went to a lefty, progressive school in Greenwich Village that had a history of teaching red-diaper babies.

My dream job at my dream school was even founded by a fellow dyke and a fellow Smithie named Elisabeth Irwin. A member of John Dewey's progressive-education circle, Irwin founded the Little Red School House in 1921 as an experiment within New York City's public school system. A believer in experiential education, her students didn't sit in neat rows. They went on field trips instead. A radical in her own right, Irwin was friends with Eleanor Roosevelt and had a partner and children before marriage equality and same-gender adoption were even policy issues.

In 1941, twenty years after starting Little Red, her students voted unanimously to name Elisabeth Irwin High School after its founder.

Twenty years after the high school opened, Angela Davis graduated from Elisabeth Irwin.

Given its radical feminist history, I knew that's where I needed to be.

Today, the school marches in the New York City Gay Pride Parade each year sporting shirts that read "Elisabeth Irwin: Founder, Educator, Mother, Lesbian."

Today, I teach courses at Elisabeth Irwin that I know I would not be able to teach in many schools, public or private: A course on feminism and activism. A course on queer writers. A course solely on Toni

Morrison. A course on memoir where the students openly write about being white, black, and brown; queer, straight, and bi; rich and poor.

My first year at LREI (Little Red School House and Elisabeth Irwin High School), I taught my first Latina lesbian teenager. She was so fierce that she brought me back to life after having been dead for so long. She woke me up. Perhaps it was because she was at risk for not graduating, it further confirmed for me that I had made the right decision in coming out to all of my students—from the freshmen to the seniors—in those first few months that I started teaching there. Alejandra proved to me that my being an out teacher allowed me to support her journey through high school in a way that was effective and true for the both of us, especially as fellow queer Latinas. Criticized and shunned by her family for staying out late and dating girls, Alejandra was the only one who was being honest with herself. She didn't care that she laughed boldly. She didn't care that she wrote boldly too. She especially didn't care that everyone could see her with her girlfriend in front of the school building.

But she had no adults in her life who supported her.

She needed a role model whose sex was brown.

Alejandra reminded me of the me I had lost when I started teaching in the schools that eventually crushed me. More than any book I could've read at Smith about being a Latina lesbian, Alejandra taught me what it actually looked like to live an authentic life.

I taught Alejandra a senior English class titled Race, Class, and Gender. It was a course I had inherited from a previous teacher who had left. By teaching this class, it seemed as if Elisabeth Irwin herself had opened my closet door.

One day, Alejandra came crying to me about not doing well during her fall trimester; she was worried she would not be able to go to college. We spoke privately in a classroom that was filled with old and well-loved books stacked from the floor to the ceiling. Many of the books were written by the very revolutionaries I looked up to. I was finally in a school that felt like home.

"Alejandra, I understand your frustrations with family and school. As Latina lesbians, we have a lot to navigate."

She smiled at me and knew. She wound up graduating at the end of the year.

I was twenty-nine with my whole brown and queer career in front of me.

I'm now thirty-nine. In these last ten years, I've received a Distinguished Fulbright to interview queer youth in Mexico. I've started my own award-winning blog, *Feminist Teacher*. I've appeared on the *Melissa Harris-Perry Show* to talk about teaching feminism and the importance of creating safe and inclusive schools. I've launched a movement with other teachers to bring women's, gender, and queer studies to K–12 education. I no longer fear being pulled into back rooms, because there are no back rooms to be pulled into. I no longer fear what's on the front page, or even the back page, because I now write my own pages. I know now that it's important to live an authentic life in order to be an authentic teacher.

I found a way and made one.

14

Visibility

Erika Cobain

ENGLISH TEACHER
Saratoga High School
Saratoga, California

After more than a decade of teaching, sometimes I still feel voiceless.

In the fall, fog covers the playground of Rivera Elementary School in Torrance, California: the far fence, the expanse of grass, and the blacktop all swirl in opaque mist. When the whistle blows, children emerge from the fog like ghosts.

First fuzzy and indistinct, invisible to the yard aides, then, smiling and clear, we grin, at our discovered superpower of invisibility and giggle back into our classrooms, with mist still clinging to our eyelashes.

I am seven, and this is my school. I am in heaven.

She calls me to her room, closes the door, flips open the flaps of a box holding the VHS tape *It's Elementary: Teaching About Gay Issues in Schools.* "I think you ordered the wrong tapes." After a pause, wide-eyed, then with dawning recognition, my BTSA (Beginning Teacher Support and Assessment) mentor teacher asks, "This is what you wanted?"

I did not want the waves of concern and awkwardness that fell between us. I was obsessively dedicated to hiding my sexual orientation. Breathless, I explain, "I saw the film in graduate school during the University of California–Santa Barbara teacher education program. . . . Yes, it is the one I want; it is a great film." I snatch the video with shaking hands and dart back to my classroom. It is 1998, my first teaching job, sixth-grade English at Beverly Vista K–8 School. I tell myself I teach more effectively from the closet, since most people assume I'm straight.

The strain on my relationship is profound. "My girlfriend just punched me in the face." The 911 operator laughed and said, "Is this a joke?" She was a girl but she hit like a man. I went to work the next day with a black eye, and my boss advised me to "leave him."

I wish I could send some experiences and relationships back into the fog. The truth is frightening: not only do more cases of domestic violence go unreported; they are often not taken seriously in the GLBT community. Threats of outing another person to keep them silent are common.

I stand in front of my students: "I am not going to talk about it." I feel ashamed, dishonest, and alone.

February 2000, Proposition 22 signs sprout along the freeway on-ramp. "Yes" votes define marriage in California as a contract only between a man and a woman. Fed up, driving home from school one day, I stop my car, rip out the sign, and hurl it into the bushes.

"How does your program help me support gay or lesbian students, or students with gay or lesbian families, in the classroom?" I ask, acutely aware that my principal and the openly gay health teacher are sitting in the seminar called "Character Counts" with me. I silently shake with frustration; the presenter ignores my question and continues to tout the virtues of this new district-wide character education program adoption.

"Let me drive you back to school," my principal offers. As she steers through traffic, she turns to me and says, "She never did answer your question, did she?" *Nope.* "You know, when I first started teaching, I had a parent complain that I shouldn't be teaching about the Holocaust because I am Jewish, that I am biased. I am a *history* teacher!" I laugh, unsure how much she knows. "You are a very private person and a good teacher; just keep doing what you are doing in the classroom."

I live far from where I teach so that no one will see my other life, where I am emerging. I am as jittery as the ocean sparkling on the water on the day of the Long Beach Pride Parade. I know one of the event coordinators, and for the first time I am marching with the teachers, behind a California Teachers Association banner proclaiming "GLBT teachers make a difference." As a news camera pans the crowd, I feel a tug on the banner. I turn just in time to see the math teacher disappear under the bandstand. Speechless, I stand alone, holding the other end of the sign. She stays hidden for the day, afraid to lose her job if someone sees her on TV. Another teacher takes up the discarded end. I grip it like a swimmer grips a lifesaver. I march on.

"I am not going to the talent show at your school unless the teachers there know who I am," my fiancée tells me quietly. My mind is a whirl. I can count five people at school who know I am gay. We have been engaged two months. We ordered the rings, so I haven't yet worn mine.

Today I slip the ring on, as I walk to the lunch room I see her: the teacher for whom nothing is a secret. "I'm engaged," I say and flash the ring. "We are trying to keep it quiet." Two minutes later, in the lunch room, I try to swallow my food. I brace for what is coming.

The principal strides in. "I hear congratulations are in order."

"What? Why?" my colleagues exclaim.

"I'm getting married," I say.

"What's his name?"

"Her name is . . ." and it happens as gently as the fog dissipates; I am completely out with my staff. I am weightless, vulnerable, like I am swerving through telephone poles, a helium balloon released from a tightly clutched hand.

The talent show performance starring all the teachers is *The Sneeches* by Dr. Seuss. I read; the vice principal rides in on a tricycle as Mr. McBean. The audience laughs. I watch my principal lead my future wife to a seat in the front row with all the teachers. As the teachers on stage cycle through Mr. McBean's "Star-On" and "Star-Off" machine, the audience laughs at the silly distinctions that make the characters believe one is better than another. The machine churns and the message to me is clear: "Not one kind of Sneech is the best on the beach"—gay, straight, lesbian, or "star-bellied," everyone is welcome here.

The staff throws us a beautiful bridal shower, tears cling to my eyelashes. I have never felt so lucky and so stupid at the same time. Why did I waste five years in the closet?

July 16, 2005, our wedding guests depart Sentinel Beach for the reception. We finish with the photographer and then, our officiant, a friend and fellow Yosemite lover, stands ready to sign our marriage license: "You don't have one?" We don't have one. It is not legal. "If that wasn't a real wedding, and that isn't a commitment, then I don't know what is."

Monday afternoon, November 3, 2008, I leave my new job early, rushing to the courthouse with my wife. We decide to register for our official marriage license before the vote on Proposition 8. As I am leaving, I see one of my students climb into the car. His moms lean out the window and cheer, "We're on our way to the courthouse. Marriage license!"

"Us too!" I wave, buoyed with a joy I cannot contain. The next day, the world looks a lot less rosy. Prop 8 passes and denies marriage rights to gay and lesbian couples in California.

It takes five hours to drive to Sacramento, and five hours to drive back. Protesting the Prop 8 decision is important. We stock up on pretzels and drinks and make our protest signs: "Love Equals Love" with a Human Rights Campaign sticker in the middle of two hearts. Soon, we stand in front of the state capitol's steps and lend our voices to making history.

"Invite your husband," my new vice principal says, "to the staff holiday party." I have to correct his assumptions. When I tell people my spouse is not "my husband," most often they say something like, "That's okay with me." This would be such an odd response to a heterosexual couple. I think I need to start using it back: *Oh, you are straight? That's okay with me.*

June 26, 2014, the class is silent, writing. My friend pokes her head into the room and whispers, "Congratulations! Did you hear? DOMA and Prop 8 were overturned!" I start to cry, grateful to have a friend who knows how much this news about the defeat of the Defense of Marriage Act means to me. This is a beautiful day. After eight years of marriage, the federal government officially recognizes me.

After more than a decade of teaching, sometimes I still feel invisible.

The last day of school, my ninth grade students sign yearbooks. I share an embarrassingly 1980s high school yearbook photo. They ask, "Who did you go to prom with, Ms. Cobain?"

"The quarterback *and* prom king," I tell them, and the football boys cheer. The conversation is identical to first period, my senior class. Except. Second period *deserves* the truth. I catch the eye of the girl who wrote about finding herself in love with another girl at summer theater camp, and then I smile at the boy who did his History Day project about gay and lesbian marriage rights. "But, know this: just like I have changed from this photo, you will change and grow, and things you believed and things you thought about yourself may change. . . . For today I am married to a woman. I have never told a whole class this before, but I am inspired by your great writing, courage, and honesty with me."

"What?" Smiles and shock and laughter, and then, the room fills with applause. What follows is a standing ovation, led by the boy who did the History Day project and the girl who loved another girl.

The shift since my colleague felt she had to flee to the anonymity of the bandstand: Gay Pride festivals are events my straight friends and their children attend. I receive a joking text, "If you are not here today at the parade, we are revoking your gay card." The PE teacher and his wife and two kids wait for me on the corner. He shouts to a marching student from his middle school Gay-Straight Alliance club. We cheer the students, the teachers, the cheerleaders, the choir, the men in gold lamé, the girls on roller skates.

Next school year, 2014–15, I will be teaching fifth grade at a feeder district for the high school. I am out with my colleagues and soon I will be out to parents and students in a community where anonymity is impossible. My wife works at the small school over the next ridge on this mountain. I drive a tree-lined road past a sign for fresh eggs and honey for sale. Everyone knows everyone. I stand on a hilltop overlooking the ocean, ridges of pine forest and auburn hills. Sometimes the fog comes in, but *today* the sky is clear to the horizon.

I am visible. I am out where I teach. I am in heaven.

15

My Story of Self-Identity

Michael Chan

CONTENT MANAGER
Huayu Education
Fuzhou, China

It has been twelve years since I left a high school teaching position for my current job in an online education company. Although I worked in the school only for the first four years after graduation from a teacher's university, I will never forget this experience, not only because it started my English teaching career but also because it began my gay life.

Unlike some of my gay friends who had a broken family or suffered from domestic violence at a younger age, I grew up in a traditional, happy family, with my father working as a civil servant, my mother a kindergarten teacher, and my elder brother a tourist agent. Perhaps influenced by my mother, I loved teaching my peers, even in primary school years, so when I had a chance to be recommended by my middle school to obtain higher education without having to endure the fierce competition of NMET (the national entrance exam to higher education), I chose Fujian Normal University to realize my teaching dream. Four years later, I graduated with distinction with an English education major and came back to teach in the same middle school where I had spent six years receiving my secondary education.

On a hot August morning in 1998, I reported to the school to meet my colleagues and gather my future students' records. It took several weeks before I became accustomed to my new role as a colleague of my former teachers. One of the most amazing things was that I met Thomas for the first time. In China's school system, an ordinary teacher normally has two roles to play simultaneously, both as an instructor of a subject and a supervisor of a class. Thomas and I suddenly became the "fathers" of sixty students (since parents in China expect the head teachers to assume their parenting responsibilities the minute their kids arrive at school), although we were not even married ourselves. Thomas and I found we had a lot in common: both of us were recommended students by middle school; we both loved swimming. The most fabulous thing was that we were even born the same day, which brought us even closer.

We exchanged our happiness and sadness about managing our students; we went swimming after class; we went shopping together for his parents as his first gift from his salary; we even chatted on the telephone after we were back home. Our relationship grew more and more intense—more than merely collegial. It felt like we were lost brothers finding each other after years of separation. We even decided to take the same training courses in order to expand our career prospects. Months later, he was accepted as my parents' third "son" after he won their great praise.

At that time, I had not yet begun my self-identification process. In my opinion then, being gay was an illness; the media demonized gay men as sissy freaks. I thought I was not sissy and certainly did not want to be treated as a freak. Therefore, I regarded Thomas as my best friend and brother, but both of us could not, and possibly would not, differentiate brotherhood and this special emotion: I felt at a loss when he was not around, and his unique giggle even at a distance away would light me up instantly. I enjoyed laying my head on his broad shoulders when sitting with him alone, even though I was much taller than he. This even became his joke about me to tell other colleagues. I loved hearing it, because he would show his proud smile whenever telling the joke and I would feel shy but happy. Every colleague liked to see the two of us brothers together, since in Chinese culture bosom brotherhood is praised and cherished.

It was not until I was asked to write this story that I realized how much I still remembered this romance. Thomas was my first love, and it was pure. We never had sexual contact. One afternoon, sleeping on his left side in my bed for a nap after lunch, I suddenly had a desire to hug him. I reached my hand for his shoulder naturally, because I anticipated he would not refuse me, but I was wrong. He pushed my hand away and turned his back to me. I did not insist, but this incident pushed me to think over our relationship. Were we best friends? Was it something more than friendship? What is that something? What is wrong with me?

I tried to search books in the library for the answer, but could not find any useful information. I realized that maybe I could get the answer from the Internet. I emptied all my savings to buy a computer and a modem (more than my annual income then) and started my online journey. Thanks to my English skills, I quickly found many gay porn sites after googling "gay." The moment I saw those nude guys, I knew all the answers to many whys that had puzzled me before then. I did not feel guilty or ashamed in the least but released and relaxed: I am who I am, and I am not alone in the world. But what about Thomas and me? I certainly fell in love with him, and my self-identity cleared up the nature of our relationship, but it swept away all the romance brought about by the vague nature of our brotherhood or friendship.

Since that afternoon, I noticed his slight changes: I received more excuses that kept him from our usual time alone; I saw him playing sports with other male colleagues. I knew I had to distance myself from him after I understood my true sexuality. He might not be gay, and he might feel pressured. Perhaps because he was an only son, the traditional concept of carrying on the family line prevented him from pursuing his own desire and sexuality. I chose to respect his choice and withdrew. We became ordinary colleagues.

During the subsequent sixteen years, Thomas married one of his colleagues and had a family of his own, while I found my true love and worked as a volunteer for a local grassroots LGBT nongovernmental organization that helped young LGBTs achieve self-identity and bridged the gap between the straight community and sexual minorities. I truly enjoy my life now and hope he does too.

16

How Far "Out" Do You Have to Be?

Dominique Gerard

DIRECTOR OF DIVERSITY AND INCLUSION
Montclair Kimberley Academy
Montclair, New Jersey

I'm struggling with what to say to you. I'm imagining you, a closeted gay teacher, reading this book. You might be like I was five years ago: still completely in the closet and not knowing even where to begin. Like me, you might be facing the end of a marriage and the terrifying idea of telling your young children about yourself, or you may be wrestling with how to tell your parents who do not support the "gay lifestyle." You might be spending a lonely afternoon in a Barnes & Noble, surreptitiously passing by the LGBTQ section and picking up this book, shoving it in between two more innocuous books, to go sit in a dark corner and pore over the pages.

You might be like I was four years ago, out to family and close friends but still keeping a lid on your story at work, worried that being out might jeopardize your career. Unlike me, you may even be in a state or country where being out might jeopardize your job or your life.

Perhaps you're like I was three years ago and consider yourself in the closet with the door open. Tucked in among the pictures on your desk, you have a picture of you and your partner, whom everyone at work has met at the holiday party. She or he may even attend the occasional choir concert or school play with you, but you always keep your distance in the theater lobby and don't introduce her or him to the students who greet you. Kids "know" about you—or at least you think they do—but you have never acknowledged your identity publicly. You say to yourself that you're open to talking about it—if a student asks you a question.

Or you may even be like I was starting two years ago. You've stood in front of your class with a lump in your throat and a pit in your stomach, looking out over a sea of students' faces and preparing yourself to say the words you thought you would never say in a classroom: "I'm gay." Wherever you are in your journey, I hope my words provide some encouragement or some comfort.

My coming-out story is inextricably tied to my school story. Soon after graduate school, I landed a job teaching history at an elite independent Northeastern day school. I moved to my school's town with my wife, who would teach English there, and our two young children, who would have the privilege of attending. Having attended large public schools in the South, my wife and I thought we had hit the jackpot. We loved our students, and they loved us. We worked long hours and took on too many additional responsibilities, but we got to work with these great students in so many different capacities. As the years progressed, I realized that I really wanted to make a career of "doing school." I went back to graduate school for an education degree, and I pushed myself to do more. I was ambitious and hardworking. I started to move up the ranks into the school's administration.

All the while, school also defined our life outside the workday too. Our students babysat our kids, and on weekends we would take them in the stroller to watch school football games. In the summer we would swim in the school's pool and host barbecues with other school families. We started a supper club and even celebrated holidays with some other faculty members and their kids. School was our life, and the people in it became our family.

Yet underneath the picture of this all-American family, I was falling apart. As cliché as it may sound, I had always known I was different since I was a young boy. I didn't put a name to it, didn't even really know the name I could give it. Growing up in Texas in the eighties, being openly gay was never a realistic option for me. I worked hard to convince myself that whatever feelings I had were a phase I would grow out of eventually. I got married at a young age to my best friend, and we had a wonderful life together. In fact, it was everything I could have wanted for myself, and for a long time we were just so busy with graduate school, jobs, and the two beautiful kids we had that it all seemed to work. But by the time we started to settle in to our lives at school and as our daughter and son became more and more independent, the veneer started to wear thin. My wife and I started to fight more and more, and all the good things that filled up our lives started to be replaced by ever-growing resentments. School and the children soon became the only things that still made us happy and bound us together. Having been a child of divorce myself, I swore that I would never end our marriage, no matter how resentful we became, no matter how unhappy it made us. Yet when my wife decided to take a new job at another school, our relationship moved into a decline that I don't think either of us could prevent. Though we struggled to put on happy faces at parties and cookouts, our anger—at each other, at ourselves, at life—was always just beneath the surface. Then one rainy morning in April 2009, after another night full of rage and resentment, we looked at each other and decided that our marriage was over. Though we did not say exactly why our marriage was ending—neither of us could be that honest with each other in that moment—we both knew it was all just too much for us to bear anymore.

I remember walking out alone into the woods near our house that day and finally saying the words I had forbidden myself from ever saying out loud: "I'm gay." No one heard it but the trees and me, but at that moment that was enough. I cried in those woods for a long time. I cried because I was so relieved but also because I felt I was failing everyone I loved. On the last day of school, we sat our children down and told them we were separating. They were devastated, but eventually came to accept the change in our lives. I would move out of our house on July 1.

Facing a long, lonely summer on my own, I had to confront the looming question that hung over my every move: What do I do now? I could finally acknowledge that I was gay to myself, but what about the rest of the world? I felt that I was too deep into the life I had

chosen at my school, too public in my constructed image as the ste-
reotypical heterosexual prep school teacher and administrator. Over
the past few years, as my personal life had become more untenable,
I had invested more of my energy into this image, and I was good
at it. I had become a full-time school administrator and was on a
definite career path. I firmly believed I was going to be a headmaster
one day. I wasn't worried that I would get fired if I came out—New
Jersey has strong workplace protections in place, as did my school. I
just couldn't let my personal disaster affect my professional goals and
aspirations. I had to be successful at *something*. But what was I supposed to do about the inconvenient fact that I was gay?

So, I ran through my options. I could come out. But whoever
heard of a gay headmaster? I could continue to be straight and re-
bound with another serious relationship as soon as possible. No, I
couldn't face the thought of that. I knew I was gay and wanted to
finally be able to date men. I even entertained the Machiavellian idea
of dating a few women publicly at school while starting to date men
on the side, but the prospect of that complicated situation was too
much for me to bear.

So, like every other LGBTQ person, I started the process of coming out, but like any good historian, I needed to do my research first.
I started to voraciously read or watch coming-out stories online, on
LogoTV, on YouTube, in bookstores. It was during one such trip to
Barnes & Noble that I found the book *One Teacher in Ten*. What an
amazing moment for me, to read the stories of teachers like me struggling with the same essential question: How do I come out with students watching? Of course, my coming-out process would be further
complicated by other questions. How do I come out to my preteen
children? How do I come out publicly while I teach their friends in
my classes? And of course, my overwhelming fear: How do I come
out and still keep moving forward in my career? I realized then the
supreme importance of having these kinds of stories available to kids
who are struggling with their identity. Watching these videos and
reading these stories started to provide me with a template, a pattern
of words that I could attach to all the crazy emotions I was feeling.

Every story was different, but the recurrent themes provided so much comfort to me. In their own unique ways, every story kept telling me, "It's all going to be okay."

In short order, I came out to my soon-to-be ex-wife, my parents, my brother, and my closest friends and colleagues. Obviously there were a lot of emotions involved—particularly for my ex-wife—but everyone was extraordinarily supportive and caring. I was in no way fully out at school, but that was okay. My personal life was—for once—personal, and no one needed to know my business. I still could not come out to my children, but I didn't feel any immediate need to do so. The trauma of divorce had been enough for them, and I saw no need to add more struggles to their lives. I realized that I could quietly continue working on my career at school and live the rest of my life privately.

However, something completely unexpected came along and disrupted my plans entirely: I fell in love. I met this great guy through an online dating service, and we hit it off. More important, he didn't care that I had two older children from my previous marriage and was excited to meet them. He wanted to be a part of my whole life, not just one sealed-off compartment of that life. Completely unprepared to come out to my kids and tell them about this new love, I went back into research mode and read up on the subject.

All the literature cautioned against coming out to middle school–age kids when they're in the midst of working out their own identity. I pondered hiding this relationship from them until they were older; perhaps I could wait until my son graduated from high school in eight years. A long period of deceit and denial stretched before me, and again it seemed like too much to bear. What would my kids think when I told them that I'd been hiding who I was for close to a decade?

After a solid month of memorizing my "coming-out speech" for my children, I sat them down and quietly recited the words I had practiced for months. When I finished, they both looked at me and said, "Well, that's okay. We still love you." After I hugged them both through my grateful and relieved tears, they asked, "Can we go back to watching TV now?" Though we would have many more conversations in the years that followed, my kids would always continue to astound me with their resilience, compassion, and love. Soon after, I introduced them to my partner over burgers and bowling, and they've been thick as thieves ever since. The concerns I had soon melted away, and I knew that everything was, in fact, going to be okay.

Over the ensuing year or so, I grew increasingly comfortable with my life in the closet with the door open at school and continued to grow as an administrator. I braved bringing my boyfriend to the school's holiday party and being more open with my colleagues. My kids were proud of my new relationship, and they started telling their close friends. I put a picture of my partner and me on my desk, along with pictures of my kids. My bosses were incredibly supportive, and my worries about my career self-destructing faded a bit more each day. Through conferences and other avenues, I was able to meet other openly gay administrators—and yes, even headmasters—and talk to them about their experiences. Undoubtedly, they met with some struggles of their own along the way, but to a person, they told me that living openly and honestly was the most important thing. Walking away from those conversations, I felt I had achieved the kind of balance these mentors were talking about. I was open and honest about who I was with my family, friends, and colleagues, and I continued to work hard as a capable and competent school administrator.

As I progressed in my own career, I started to focus on diversity and inclusion. I put a sign on my door, "Safe Space," which designated my office as a place where anyone could come in to talk with me. For years our school had no out LGBTQ students, but I felt certain that with all the effort and time I was putting into diversity and inclusion programming at my school, these kids would feel comfortable coming out now. But nothing happened. I thought I was doing everything I could to promote inclusion, but clearly I wasn't. In my desire to be successful, I signed up for a weeklong summer diversity leadership program. It was in a session late in the week that I truly understood why I was there and the work I really needed to do.

I took an assessment that asked me a number of questions regarding communication and conflict. I asked our facilitator, "Does this mean how I communicate at home or at school?" She looked perplexed, so I elaborated: "When I'm communicating at home, I'm very emotional and demonstrative. I raise my voice, I cry sometimes, I laugh a lot, and I get frustrated and sad. But when I'm at school, my first priority is to be competent and in control, so I react to emotional situations and conflict with a great deal of restraint." She told me she didn't really have an answer for me, but that I should do the best I can with the assessment. As I started answering the questions, I grew increasingly frustrated and actually started to tear up. After all I had been through over the last few years, I thought I had come out on the other side as a whole, fully evolved human being. I was in a relationship, my kids loved me, I was finally happy. So why was I now sitting in front of a stupid questionnaire unable to answer simple questions about myself? When our facilitator came over to me again and saw the pain I was going through, I told her, "I just don't know how to answer." And she said the simple wise thing I needed to hear in that moment, "I think that's your answer. You need to work more on you." As I thought about it more and more, I realized the road-block for me personally and professionally: I couldn't truly be myself at school until I came out to my students.

There exist several schools of thought on the issue of coming out to your students. Many people say you shouldn't share your personal life with students. Others argue that if you are gay and come out, then you needlessly politicize your classroom. When I looked back on my own schooling now as an adult, I realized that all along the way I had gay teachers in my life. My elementary school vice principal, my fourth-grade reading teacher, my fifth-grade math teacher, my seventh-grade history teacher, my eighth-grade theater teacher, and my high school speech and debate coach—all of them were gay men. I wasn't particularly close to every single one of them, but every step of the way on my journey I had these men in my life.

I knew even then that I shared something in common with them, but I never would have come to them, never would have shared anything personal about my own struggles with them. A barrier always existed between us, and I think it's because not a single one of them was out. Again, I went to school in Texas in the eighties, and I don't blame them for staying closeted. But here I was, trying to make a difference in how a school felt for kids who were silenced for any number of reasons. How could I hope to get them to stand up and speak out about their experiences if I remained silent about my own?

So, I developed a get-to-know-you exercise for the first week of school that I called "Points of You." On a blank sheet of paper, I asked students to list at least fifteen words that describe who they are. After that, I asked them to outline the descriptors that they are most known by in school, underline the descriptors that they are most proud of, give some rays to the single most surprising descriptor about themselves, and box in the descriptors that most people don't know or that they might be uncomfortable with people knowing. To give them an example, I filled out a "Points of You" for myself, and I included the words *gay* and *partner*. I thought this exercise would be a great way to establish a safe environment in my class where both my students and I could feel open about who we were.

Conceptually, this was all well and good, but when the day came to actually do the "Points of You" exercise, I was a nervous wreck. Though I had gotten approval for my exercise from my boss and talked it over with my own kids, I still felt apprehensive. What if parents got upset? What if my students laughed? What if they said something mean to my kids who walked the halls with them? As I introduced the exercise, my palms started to sweat and I grew short of breath. My classroom seemed to get inexplicably smaller and hotter. After they filled out their sheets, I told them that I wanted to share my own "Points of You." I projected my sheet up on the screen, and I held my breath. After a few seconds of silence, I told them the following:

> I want to share with you what I wrote, because I don't think it would be fair to ask you to take any kind of risk sharing with me if I won't take a risk myself. Some of the identifiers I have up there may be surprising to you—like the fact that I'm gay—and I want to tell you why I'm sharing them with you. When I grew up in Texas, I only ever heard two things about gay people. I heard about gay people when

our TV news would report on the city's Pride parade and I saw people in crazy costumes and watched the news anchors laugh. And I heard about gay people during Sunday school where we learned that those kinds of people were going to hell. I'm sure your experience has been really different, and you have a much more complex understanding of what it means to be gay. That being said, you still might not know a gay person in real life, and I feel like it's important that you do. Gay people are still often stereotyped or caricatured in the media, and I'd like you to know that I'm all those other things on my "Points of You" sheet—I'm Hispanic, I'm a teacher, a parent, a singer, a bad dancer, a son who loves his parents, and a person who struggled with ADHD as a student. I'm all these things and a lot more. Gay people are just as complicated as everyone else, and I want you to know that being gay can't possibly define everything a person is.

I also want to tell you about my identity because I heard my friends use homophobic language all the time as an insult when I was growing up. And you and I both know that terms like "That's so gay" and other uglier slurs still get used in this school all the time. I think it's important that you know those terms insult people like me. Much more important, you should know that they are probably hurting some of your classmates. The tough thing about homophobic language—as opposed to racist language—is you more often don't see or know the people you are hurting. But I'm here. We're here. When you hear that hurtful language, I want you to think of me. Those words hurt real people.

I also just want you to know that I value and respect anything you do or don't want to share with me on your "Points of You" sheet. I hope you know that this classroom is a safe space where you and I can both be ourselves.

Some students smiled slyly as I spoke, others nodded quietly, and some even looked kind of bored. And that was okay. I was out—fully and completely. I didn't realize the enormous weight I still carried on my shoulders until that moment. In that moment, I realized what it meant to be truly open and honest. It was such a relief.

Over the few years that I've done this "Points of You" exercise, students have shared some incredibly poignant and important moments with me regarding their identities, experiences, and families, and I have been humbled by their honesty and courage. Knowing their stories has made me a better teacher and a better advocate for kids and families who may not feel they have a voice in our community. And wouldn't you know, kids started coming to my office, too! I won't say that they visit my office because I'm openly gay, but I think that being more relaxed and open about who I am is reflected in the work I do. My office still has a "Safe Space" sign on the door, and it finally is a safe space for everyone who enters it, even me.

PART 3

The Struggle Continues

17

Teacher of the Year

Brett Bigham

SPECIAL EDUCATION TEACHER

Portland, Oregon

The crowd was roaring as we rode into Memorial Coliseum. Behind us marched a kilted bagpipe band. There were balloons and flags and banners and arms waving in the air. Suddenly the Volkswagen-sized speakers blared out, "Ladies and Gentlemen, give a warm welcome to Brett Bigham, the 2014 Oregon State Teacher of the Year! He is the first special education teacher to be given this award! Riding with him is his husband, Mike Turay, in a 2015 Chevrolet Camaro convertible!"

I hear a slight moan out of my incredibly shy husband, precariously perched next to me on the back of the convertible, so I did what I had to do. I gently (I hope) elbowed him in the ribs and growled through my giant smile, "Wave, honey!" And we began waving at the first of the two hundred thousand people lined up along the almost four-hour route of the Portland Rose Festival's Grand Floral Parade.

Every four blocks or so there was a scaffold towering above the crowds with more gigantic speakers and a local news celebrity announcing us to the next few blocks of bleachers and seats, which were crammed with over a fifth of the city's population lining up to see the parade. Every four blocks we got to watch the crowd as they processed the announcement. Cheers, waving, shouting at the Teacher of the Year part; confused looks, frozen waves, and shock at the husband part.

I couldn't help wondering, How had a special ed teacher ended up on the back of a convertible with his husband of five days, breaking new ground in America as one of the first openly gay teachers of the year? It felt a little bit like *The Twilight Zone.*

Portland is a liberal island of blue floating in the sea of red that is the bulk of Oregon. Being an openly gay teacher in Portland is not a big deal. It's not something I've ever discussed with students, but my coworkers are adults and they know who I go home to.

So becoming Teacher of the Year in a state where most of the geography is Republican red means that I became the representative for a whole lot of teachers who might be a whole heck of a lot more conservative than I am. I made a decision early on that I would visit every county in my state.

I wanted to get a message out to families and kids with special needs in those far-flung corners of the state that they have a champion trying to get them some love on the state and national level of education policy making. I teach kids with some of the greatest needs in our state. I'm county-level special education, and that means a student comes to me only if the local districts haven't figured out how to be successful with them. Some come my way because of medical fragility—I have two full-time nurses working out of my room. But you can almost guarantee that if a student goes into foster care and has complex needs, he will be sent to Portland and could very well end up in a class like mine.

These are the kids I'm looking out for—and then the Teacher of the Year thing happens. After my nomination from a coworker, the state asked me to do the next step: the application process. This meant a lot of essay writing and a lot of background checking. Mike and I were linked on Facebook as domestic partners, so I knew it would be only a matter of time before that bubbled up to the surface. I didn't really expect to win. Special ed teachers don't win those big awards, and the fact I was openly gay, I was sure, was a can of worms the state wasn't willing to open.

But I like to plan ahead, and so I thought, "What if?" I sat Mike down and we had a long talk. Domestic partner to domestic partner. Outgoing, comfortable-in-the-spotlight domestic partner to shy domestic partner. I told Mike that if this were to happen, it would be groundbreaking and a big step in the world of LGBT rights, as well as a milestone in special ed. I looked him in the eye and said, "You'll have to be in the Gay Pride Parade." He blanched about the color of our white kitten, Montecore, but with a trembling voice said, "I'd do that."

My heart swelled up because I domestically partnered one heck of a peach, because he understands the power of standing as a couple in a situation like that. The caption of the photo, in a case like that, says it all: "Teacher of the Year and his domestic partner." And if you're a confused LGBT teenager in a faraway corner of Oregon who sees that, then you know you're not the only one. You know LGBT kids can grow up to become teachers. You see that there are places in Oregon where you can have a partner and be open about it without fear. This is the role I get to play just by being myself: Mike gets to be the eye candy on my arm. But we didn't think I'd win, so we didn't think we would really need to deal with it.

When my phone rang and I heard the voice at the other end announce that I was a finalist, I was flabbergasted. A few weeks later my superintendent walked me into the auditorium to "show me a new coffee cart" the school had purchased. Thinking nothing of her somewhat unusual request, I was shocked to see my coworkers, my students, and the media all lying in wait for me. Oregon had its first special education teacher as Teacher of the Year. As I sat on the stage and people gave speeches about me, my mind was whirling. I had been looking online and found no mention of any gay Teachers of the Year from any state, but I had been told that at least three of us had, over the years, won the award. I might not be the first, but I was guessing I might be the most out one. I stumbled through an acceptance speech and sweated through a couple of TV and radio interviews. This was getting interesting fast.

And the same thoughts kept going through my head. I knew I was going to keep some kids from committing suicide. In high school, my best buddy told me one day that he couldn't figure out dating girls and that it wasn't for him. He was distraught and upset, but it seemed like no biggie to me. I'd come to that conclusion about myself years prior. I figured we were just gonna be best *gay* buddies now. I called and checked up on him a few times, but he didn't answer, so I just left messages. Finally I decided I'd left enough messages and it was his turn to call me. It turned out that my best buddy had walked out to his driveway, sat on the hood of his car, put a shotgun in his mouth, and killed himself. His mom found him lying back on the hood of his station wagon. Gone.

I was already at school when I found out.

I was fifteen. He was dead. I didn't go to his funeral. I didn't call his parents. I never saw them again. I'm the only one who knows why he did it, and I didn't have the guts to tell his parents. Not that he was giving up on girls, but that I hung up the phone.

Now back to the parade. Perhaps you'll understand what riding in that parade meant. Two hundred thousand people lining up, that many more at home watching on TV, but all of them hearing that same message: "Riding with him is his husband, Mike." You see, I can never go back to 1980 and undo what happened with my buddy. I can't tell my friend that he has an amazing future ahead of him. But what I can do is sit tall in the back of that Camaro, I can wave and smile and feel my husband's leg up against mine as we slip and cling for four hours, trying not to slide off the back of that glossy black car in front of the whole city.

Just us being there together on that hot day in June was message enough. If you are gay, there are better options than suicide. You can be a husband. You can be a teacher. You can be Teacher of the Year. You can be on a float in one of the country's largest parades. You can just be.

But this amazing experience has not been all parades and cheering crowds. Following one of my first speeches, a supervisor in my department said, "You need to watch what you say. You need to stop saying you are gay. Someone is going to kill you." I was stunned. "Someone is going to kill you," she repeated. "Someone is going to shoot you in the head."

At the time I just thought she was being dramatic, but soon after I was called into a meeting with her and the department head and given this somewhat chilling directive. I was no longer allowed to write or speak as Teacher of the Year unless the district had approved what I was going to say. "And you are *always* Teacher of the Year," added the supervisor who had told me to stop saying I was gay.

After that, these supervisors began to harass and bully me. When Mike and my mother came to the district board meeting I was honored at, the four people above me in my department sat in the row in front of us. My supervisor was a mere two inches from my knees. They never turned around and acknowledged we were there. They never said hello to Mike or my mom. My department never announced I was Teacher of the Year. The head of special education never said a word to me about it. It was a chilly reception, to say the least.

I traveled to Washington for the ceremony honoring all the state Teachers of the Year. My pride was sullied by the fact that I was meeting President Obama with a gag order in place. Here I was, standing in the White House, being given one of the highest teaching honors in the United States, and if I say anything about being gay, I've been told I'll be written up at work. Here I had the chance to be the voice for so many. In my briefcase were the statistics of gay teen suicides. My heart was breaking; I was thinking I would not be able to stand up for those kids. Following the ceremony, the teachers were surrounded by the White House press corps, and we were asked if anyone wanted to make a statement. I struggled. But then I thought of my friend and those phone calls and how I always regretted not speaking up. So I pushed by the Teacher of the Year from Georgia, saying, "Pardon me, I am coming out of the closet." I walked up to the microphones and said:

> As one of the first openly gay Teachers of the Year I am so pleased to be sending a message to our gay youth that there is a future ahead of them. Thirty percent of all teen suicides are by gay youth, and these laws that we're passing across the states that demean gay people and make our youth feel terrible about themselves need to stop.

It wasn't until later that I realized what I had done. I put my job in jeopardy, but I had stood my ground. I knew the gag orders were illegal, but I figured I had just made enemies out of the people I worked with. My White House statement was my shot across their bow. I would not be silenced. This time I would stay on the phone and not hang up. There are LGBT kids considering suicide. Nobody was going to stop me from talking to them.

A few weeks later Oregon began allowing gay marriages, and Mike and I headed to the courthouse as soon as school was over. We had been waiting for years to get married in our home state and now was our chance. I put an update on Facebook—"We're getting married today!"—and headed downtown. The media was waiting on the courthouse steps for me. There was a reporter from the local paper and a videographer. They were going to follow us from start to finish and there wasn't much we could say about it.

My shy husband-to-be arrived, and we got in line to get our license. It was a festive atmosphere, with the community there in support. One family had come in with buckets of roses and they were giving everyone getting married a rose. The lesbian choir kept breaking into "Going to the Chapel." Mike glowed red with embarrassment. We walked seven blocks to where the ceremony was being held, and the media walked with us, filming us the entire way. A local group who had been fighting for marriage rights had rented a hall and were performing marriages on the spot. When we walked in they pulled me aside and told us they had a private room for us to be married in. No media was allowed.

Though we were promised privacy, the news crews refused to leave. I let Mike make the choice. Either we got married on live TV, or we had to leave and find someone else to do the ceremony. Mike understood the importance of what was happening. He knew the message we would send to LGBT youth by giving up our privacy. So we got married in the glare of the lights and the sound of camera shutters going off all around us. There was no walking down the aisle as a married couple: the microphones and cameras were shoved in our faces and we could hardly take a step. Mike did interview after interview and was a real trooper. The videos were up on the news stations before we even left the building. My mom saw it on TV before we had a chance to tell her.

As we left the building, married, another round of media was laying in wait. We stepped over cables and moved from reporter to reporter. And then it was behind us, we were alone on the street. I looked at Mike and grinned. "You did a good job, honey." He gave me this long look. I know he was reeling from what had just happened. "That was important," he said, and took my hand. We walked back to the car in silence. After so many years, we were able to be married. We had to share our day with the public, something neither of us had wanted to do, but the thought of the kids who would see the headlines and the news stories was a consolation. Our marriage was more than a commitment to each other. It was an example for the country.

A few days later came the Rose Festival parade in Portland. A week after that came a letter from President Obama. The White House staff had been interested in me even before I came to Washington. (I had learned this in the most unsubtle of ways: as I entered the vice president's mansion for the Teacher of the Year luncheon, one of Vice President Biden's staff members read my credentials and shouted out, "Oregon! You're the gay one! We're all following you on Facebook!") But I did not expect the president of the United States to take the time to send us a letter of congratulations. The White House understood the importance of that letter. It had arrived wrapped in layers of cardboard and the message was clear: This letter is an important historical document.

And somehow, on the eve of the fiftieth anniversary of the Civil Rights Act, just a month after our wedding, I found myself on the Mall in Washington, DC, standing at the base of the Martin Luther King Jr. Memorial, giving a speech about equality and freedom. I spoke about how many of our LGBT kids end their struggles with suicide. I thought of my friend Mark, sitting on the hood of his white station wagon in his driveway back in 1980, and I knew that if he had heard me speak, he wouldn't have done it. I spoke to him and all those LGBT kids who have ended things too soon. But, mostly, I spoke to the ones who are still here. "Look at what you can do!" was my message. "There is a future! Hang in there; I've got your back."

As I write this, I've just passed the two-thirds mark in my year of service as Teacher of the Year. I have already participated in one national panel and have been asked to keynote at two more. Two weeks ago the *New York Times* interviewed me because Secretary of Education Arne Duncan credited me as one of the teachers who had helped him change his mind on national policy. This past Saturday I attended my 175th event as Teacher of the Year. My voice is being heard. People know about my kids with special needs, and LGBT kids are hearing they can grow up to be a teacher.

But my district continues to try and silence me. I am on my second gag order. You'll notice I have not said where I work. I have been told I will be put on administrative leave if I do. I have to apply three weeks in advance now for any appearance as Teacher of the Year. My supervisor will decide if I can appear as Teacher of the Year or as a private citizen. The three events this year for LGBT youth outreach—introducing the LGBT teen choir at a concert on a Sunday, meeting with the LGBT center about bullying, and the local high school Gay-Straight Alliance—were all denied. I have had to file a grievance with the union as I refuse to follow their gag order. I refuse to turn in my speeches for them to edit. I refuse to turn in this essay for their approval.

You see, when I was fifteen I made a mistake. I hung up the phone. Now I have a chance to speak that message to every LGBT kid in my state. I will not be silenced.

18

The Advocate

Esih Efuru

ENGLISH INSTRUCTOR
The Lincoln School
Charlotte, North Carolina

I approached the summer of 2014 with gratitude and joy. My child-hood dream of becoming an educator had been molded by a thou-sand joys and aches. My journey from Newark, New Jersey, to the South in 2004 was one for the Lifetime channel. Then I made my way through teaching middle school eighth grade, the depression of a lay-off in 2011, and the joy of a return to teaching in 2014 with battle scars that shone like stars. I had no complaints; I'd made the most of the magic and was now living the dream as an English teacher. My bundle of creativity, mother wit, and motivation yielded sneaky grins of ad-miration from adventurous adolescents and warm smiles of support from curious educators and administrators.

As the testing window approached, students groaned and teach-ers pushed, both exhausted from countless hours of review and re-minders. Finally, students were left to their mornings of truth while we prayed for high scores. After lunch, we teachers escorted students to the gymnasium for a break from daily assessments. Here and there, we'd supervise gossip circles, lovebirds, and music ciphers and check in on the loners who preferred to observe the camaraderie from a dis-tance. On one of these long, hot June afternoons, I noticed a few male students off to the side teasing classmates and simulating dance moves familiar in "the ball scene," where gay male participants proudly saunter down runways in haute couture and twist their bodies to syn-copated house-music rhythms. I smiled and remembered my own days on those spirited catwalks, where the boy in me winked at the ladies and high-fived the drag queens with glorious pirouettes of pride along the velvet walkway.

The young men beamed at one another and shared soft compli-ments without care of the crowd. As I sat on the bench nearby, sev-eral teachers struck up a debate about whether or not homosexuality was genetic or learned behavior. The teachers slyly critiqued the boys' mannerisms during their exchanges, blind to caution. I pondered whether or not to interject, having resolved in my first weeks as a new team member to leave my orientation status at home.

My heart dropped as the conversation went on, and my face dampened as I tried to focus on the interactions between the kids on the basketball court and bleachers. I insisted on removing myself from the room and floating in my mind to a happy place, but my thoughts kept me hostage in this moment of humiliation. The adults smiled and conjectured that female-run homes and high levels of sen-sitivity caused homosexuality, inferring that it was a character defect.

A knot formed in my stomach as I remembered my college years, when students rallied together to protest the "establishment" of rac-ism on campus but harassed and ostracized the gay students as we entered parties, dining halls, and dorm lounges. An instant headache crept up just as a colleague offered his explanation that homosexual-ity was not born within but rather learned and that the Bible supports the eradication of this spirit of "confusion."

Audre Lorde's infamous quote, "Your silence will not protect you," sang around my ears as I listened on. While I charged others to live boldly and courageously from the pulpit and in my social circles, I now stood at the crossroads of truth and justice. Could I, an openly gay reverend and mother, trade insult for comfort and still walk proud? I'd just heard a sermon by the Reverend Russell Thornhill of Unity Fellowship Church in Los Angeles about being the sole voice of justice for the many that are silent through oppression. I could honor my personal illusion of safety and stay mute, or I could step forward and offer a beam of light to a cloud of dark notions.

As staff members exchanged bigoted clichés, I gently interjected and challenged them to consider life on a case-by-case basis. My heart quickened as I declared my orientation and passionately shared my own story. Although I boldly detailed my history, I panicked internally and thought I had just terminated myself. However, I just couldn't stop advocating for acceptance. As scared as I was to share the truth, I was determined to rebuke the judgment being passed around the room. I pushed worry to the back of my mind and kept on stressing the importance of love and respect. My hands shook as I spoke, but I could not stop the flow of truth. It didn't matter at the time how I felt; what mattered was that the individuals listening to me were clear that it wasn't okay to impose their contrived theories on others because of their own homophobia. I was willing, whether I felt good about it or not, to sacrifice myself for the good of the students around me, who deserved to make their own choices in spite of the criticisms of others. I had to remember the pain of what was forced on me and do what I could to prevent that from happening to another child. If I lost my job, then it meant that I was there long enough to make the impact that God intended. I trusted God more than myself and went forward.

I went on to have an intense but productive dialogue with the leader of the conversation, who was also a pastor, in which we exchanged spiritual truths and scriptures before settling on the fact that a movement of love and faith is what we all desire to be a part of. As we all departed the gymnasium, I looked upon the youngsters, who passed me with warm hugs and held my eyes knowingly as I nodded my acceptance. My heart and my spirit both shivered for a second as I realized the power in that moment of knowledge and justice, a moment where love became the victorious advocate. There would be more battles in the war, but on that particular afternoon the hope within me illuminated my entire being. I walked a little taller on my commute home that day, and though I was a bit anxious about how my colleagues would handle my coming out, I felt both relieved and proud that I had potentially prevented an act of intolerance. Perhaps a child would not be mocked tomorrow; maybe another teacher would think before he or she spoke. I was humbled that love had provided me an opportunity to be the advocate for the silenced and seemingly invisible, and was further committed to being a beacon of light for LGBTQ students who needed a place to call home.

19

Good Enough?

"Mr. G"

HIGH SCHOOL GUIDANCE COUNSELOR
Bronx, New York

"What's wrong?" I asked "Lisa." She was one of my students with whom I usually spoke about classes and graduation requirements and music and pop culture. Today our discussion would be different. As she stared down at her white Jordans, she explained her problem. Her mother had learned that she had a girlfriend. (In fact, it was a staff member who had outed her.) This was unacceptable in her mother's eyes; she did not approve of Lisa being a lesbian. Her mother, a devout Christian, believed that religion would "cure" her daughter. Lisa was forced to attend church, to alter her appearance, and to change the music she listened to. It was a traumatic experience for Lisa as her identity was squashed. While still the same girl who worked diligently in school and never got in trouble, at home Lisa was treated like a criminal who needed to be reformed.

As our conversation continued, my heart hurt because I could see her pain. As her guidance counselor, I knew my primary role was to console and assist her. I wondered if she knew I was gay, would it make her feel better? I was pretty sure it would, but I elected not to tell her about myself. Instead, I said, "Lisa, you do whatever makes you happy." I told Lisa that I supported her and said, "You should date whomever you want." She halfheartedly accepted my response, but it was evident that she felt alone. I knew that feeling all too well. Our conversation concluded and the lock on my closet remained tightly secure. I did not feel satisfied with our discussion. It could have been so impactful; we could have commiserated about some of the individual challenges that we each face due to our sexuality and discussed some strategies on how to best handle these disheartening situations. Unfortunately, that part of the conversation never occurred.

Can I teach my students to stand up to bullies, become honest individuals, and be true to themselves if I am not true to myself and to them? Beyond that, is it even my responsibility to come out as a gay man to the school, the staff, and the students? To fully understand the predicament I am in, it is important to understand more about my school. While a handful of educators are out to some of the staff, no adult is out to the students. From the teachers to the janitors, to the people who serve sloppy joes at lunch, if they are gay, the students do not know. It feels as if our school culture promotes a "don't ask, don't tell" policy, because being gay is just not talked about. We do not have LGBT speakers, visible posters that encourage tolerance of different sexual orientations, any acknowledgement of LGBT History Month in October, or an active Gay-Straight Alliance. The acceptance of individuals with different sexual orientations and gender identities is simply not there, neither among staff nor students.

Hearing the word "faggot" or the phrase "that's gay" in the hallways, cafeteria, and gymnasium is certainly a common occurrence. It makes me wonder why students are rarely held accountable for using these words. If I hear students say one of these obscenities, they are addressed. I wish more adults in the building would respond in a similar manner, because as educators it is important for us to teach moral values such as acceptance and tolerance. The LGBT student population hears these taunts, whether directly or indirectly. I know it upsets them, and I also know that some students are openly gay. They display the fortitude to be themselves and act incredibly courageous in the face of these insults. I remain a coward and stay closeted, even though I know perceptions and stereotypes could change if I did come out. (I am not implying that anyone who is not out is a coward. However, when I compare myself to those individuals who risk harassment, ridicule, and bullying for being open about their sexuality, I do feel that *I* am acting cowardly.) This certainly makes me question if I could be the best guidance counselor possible without ever breaking out of my securely locked closet.

I also realize being outed would prevent me from remaining in control of my coming-out process. I could accidentally see a former student or even a parent or a teacher at a gay bar or on a dating app or website. My worst fear would be having my sexuality cyberblasted on Instagram or Facebook. After a simple click of an iPhone, the entire school could know. Then it could be perceived that I was hiding my sexuality and that there is something wrong with being gay. Obviously, there is nothing wrong with being gay, but sometimes perception is reality and people might assume that there was something wrong with it. More important, it would rob me of the chance to speak up and come out on my own.

I have the privilege of working in a state where antidiscrimination laws protect employees regardless of their sexual orientation. Through our teachers union, I have even attended a few meetings for LGBT educators. Therefore, it would be safer for me compared to someone in twenty-nine other states, where an employee can be fired for being gay. I am adored by my students and popular among the faculty and parents. Be that as it may, students and teachers are mostly unaware of my sexuality. One of my biggest concerns is how I would be treated by the parents. Will they approve of my speaking with their child because, in their ill-conceived view, talking to them might make them gay, as if it were a contagious disease? I know that a parent like Lisa's would certainly disparage me and my credibility as a counselor. Similarly, I could be questioned and asked to justify why I called a specific student to my office. In addition, I worry about having teachers refuse to work with me because of my "lifestyle." Perhaps they would spread false rumors or make derogatory remarks about me or homosexuality or both. This type of ignorance and bigotry would be devastating. Who would be my ally? Being the only openly gay educator in the building would be a very challenging position. I would be vulnerable to being called a faggot, which would be tremendously hurtful. I would not want the students, faculty, and staff to trust and respect me less. It would be as if I was given a label, which would be hard to rip off. Anxiety. Fear. Pain. Shame. These words run through my head.

It is wishful thinking, but I just want to be judged on my personality, character, and merits. Is this not what every gay, lesbian, bisexual, or transgender person wants, considering how we have been discriminated against, criminalized, marginalized, and persecuted in the past? The only label I want to wear is one that says, "I want to be treated just like a human being."

Due to my desire to keep this secret, my relationships with colleagues have deeply suffered. I have placed a wall between myself and the majority of the staff. I have abstained from having them learn much about me and have omitted significant parts of my life. I know how to deflect questions, evade answers, and change the focus of the conversation away from myself. By not providing much information, I have expected simply to be viewed as someone who keeps his personal life separate from work. In the end, this has been completely exhausting and incredibly isolating. Too much of my mental energy has focused on hiding who I am. I carefully filter words about my social life and even wonder if I use my hands too much when speaking! Would it be "too gay"? There certainly has been no mention of my affinity for Lady Gaga and Beyoncé.

That was my situation for so many years.

Finally, the pressure of hiding my sexuality at work while dealing with other life challenges became unbearable. It resulted in me having a breakdown in front of one of my best friends at school. She tried to console me, but the isolation, stress, and pressure were too intense. I cried. It was the first time in our long relationship that she had seen tears crawl from my eyes. We spoke for a while about some of my issues, including work stress and physical ailments. My secret remained hidden. However, soon after, I realized I could not go on living like this. I needed an ally at work.

One day I called her and asked if I could come over. Upon entering her house, we quickly began chatting about school and other trivial matters. I was stalling. While I sat on a soft couch in her strongly lit living room, I held a can of flavored seltzer. The perspiration on my forehead easily surpassed the condensation on the can. Looking everywhere but at her eyes, I knew the truth needed to be told.

"I have something to tell you. Well . . . Umm . . . Well, I don't date girls anymore."

"Huh, what? What are you saying?" she asked and appeared confused.

I opened my arms, with my palms facing toward the ceiling and said, "Yeah, it's true."

"Wait. What is? Are you saying you're gay? No, you aren't." Completely perplexed, she continued, "Are you lying to me? Wha . . . Wha . . . What? You are lying. Are you kidding? Don't joke about this."

"Yup, I'm not kidding."

She eventually calmed down, and I answered many of her questions. It was a shock to her and she "needed time." When I left, I began processing what had transpired. Although I was a little disappointed by her reaction, I was extremely happy that I had told her. It was a cathartic moment, one that I will never forget. After a few hours, I returned and she apologized and said she would always support and love me. Our relationship flourished, and the friendship quickly grew. This made me ecstatic, because I knew that every day I stepped into school, I would have someone I could go to for help, advice, and, most important, to be myself. It was an incredible feeling. I had come out to one faculty member.

Two years went by and my coming-out process continued. I decided to tell another good friend in school. I felt that our friendship was evolving, but we could never be close if he did not know about my sexuality. After throwing a baseball around in the park, we went for lunch. I finally said, "You know those softball tournaments I play in? Well, they are a part of a gay league." "Fernando" was immediately shocked but happy that I had told him the truth. I felt wonderful and so relieved. Fernando surprised me by asking to play in the next softball tournament. I said, "Absolutely." The league is inclusive, and we welcome everyone. A few months later, he was quickly welcomed by the team. Although we lost some games that weekend, I came back a winner. Going to school the next day would be that much easier. Two teachers now knew.

During the most recent school year, I have come out to two more of my colleagues. Their responses have also been warm, friendly, and supportive. It feels so empowering to have allies who treat me like I deserve to be treated. In fact, everyone whom I have come out to—friends, family, and colleagues—has been extremely positive. It really makes me wonder if I should just do it. Although I am uncertain whether or not coming out at school is necessary, I continue to strive to be the best guidance counselor I can. I just hope it's enough. And I hope it was good enough for Lisa.

20

There Is Uncertainty, but There Is Also Hope

Sophie E. Gilbert

ENGLISH AND THEATER TEACHER
Riverdale High School
Riverdale, California

Over winter break, I found myself looking at the garage through the kitchen window of my home. My thoughts were of getting into the car and running it inside the garage with the door closed. I wondered how long it would take, and whether there was enough time before my wife returned home. I wondered if it would even work, so I searched "carbon monoxide poisoning" on Google. If I was going to do it, I wanted it to be successful. I had to end the horrible misery that followed me throughout my life.

In past years, I had similar thoughts when I saw a knife or a bottle of pills. The first time was when I was in high school, but I removed myself from the misery by dropping out and passing the GED exam. From there, I went to a state university where I focused on my studies, and the misery seemed to be gone. Mostly gone. I kept myself sheltered, with few friends and stacks of books. Eventually I earned two degrees and found my way back to high school, this time as a teacher. By then I was married and had a daughter. The beast was tamed. Or so I thought.

Marriage and my career were supposed to drive away those old feelings that I had been born a girl with a boy's body, those feelings I never spoke about with anyone. I chose to move forward as a husband, a father, and a male role model for my students. That was what I told myself then. But instead of the misery ending, I found myself caught in an emotional firestorm. In my first year of teaching at a public school, students and even colleagues thought I was lying when I said that I was married. Sexual innuendos and slurs implying that I was gay swirled around me on campus. It felt like everyone was laughing in my face. Somehow I survived, made it through, but I left when the school year ended.

The horrible treatment I received drove me to reexamine my past. I searched the Internet and started learning about gender dysphoria, a condition in which the brain and the body do not align regarding gender. Reading about it caused me to remember all the times as a child when I wrapped a towel around my head to simulate long hair or around my waist to simulate a skirt. When I hated the way I looked. When I felt lost or uncomfortable around other boys. When I had cuts on my face from trying to shave even more closely. I never told anyone, yet I was reading about it. My surfing in search of answers became an obsession. The answer kept coming up the same: I was transgender.

Breaking the silence frightened me, but I had to do it. My wife and I had not been married very long and telling her was risky. One day I opened up to her, telling her my entire story. It actually brought us closer. She had also been noticing things about me she did not understand, and my revelation made sense. She became my greatest ally. In subsequent stints as a teacher, she coached me on my mannerisms and expressions that people might regard as feminine. I also sought out a gender therapist and started exploring my feminine side. Both strategies served me well for many years. Expressing my feminine side in private and masking it in public helped me thrive as a teacher and develop the many skills I needed to reach young people. For a time, I served as a department head and developed curriculum. But then the day came during winter break when I found myself staring at the garage thinking about ending my life.

People who contemplate suicide do not necessarily want to die. They want to end the pain. They become desperate and lose hope.

While I had been successful as a teacher, I still occasionally got the subtle comments and innuendos that told me I was not masking my feminine side enough. The cross-dressing I did in private helped some, but the gender dysphoria became stronger the older I became. In the previous year, an at-risk student had called me a faggot in front of the class, causing students to laugh. I quit and went to a different high school. The crisis hit halfway through my first year there, after another incident in which two boys posted a picture of me on the Internet with phallic symbols drawn all over it.

No matter what I did, no matter where I went, I was never free of the humiliation of being myself. If I had to continue to be the way I was, I did not want to live. I knew what I had to do to continue living, but it was overwhelming to even think about. I needed to transition and live as a woman, but I had no idea if I was strong enough to pull it off.

After talking it over with my wife, I got myself back into counseling. It did not take long for me to earn approval to begin hormone therapy to feminize my body. The process would take place gradually over the next few years. Within a week, my skin started to become soft, and after two I started noticing sensitivity in the breast area. My face changed and took on a more feminine appearance. I had time, but I needed to prepare for the day when I would need to come out at work and live as my authentic self. I was not yet finished with my first year in my district, and I would not receive tenure until I had taught there for two years. With tenure, I would have greater protection, but the question that concerned me was how students, parents, colleagues, and the administration would treat me.

Around that time, another teacher in a nearby district transitioned. She was outed to the press, which widely publicized her transition. People in the community threatened her, spat on her, and called her a pedophile. I had the opportunity to meet her at an LGBT Pride event, and though she had a rough time, she was happy to finally live as herself. I had read about another teacher who committed suicide after being outed in a similar way. I knew it was possible for a teacher to transition and be an effective teacher, but I was not sure how my district would respond.

Living as a woman at home and a man at work has its pitfalls. Most of us do not need to think ahead about daily routines like which bathroom to enter or adjusting the pitch and resonance of one's voice to fit the gender presentation at the moment. Eventually my developing breasts would start to show, and I needed to think about what to wear to hide them. Going full time, though, would mean standing in front of teenagers all day, every day as a woman, and I needed to allow myself time for the hormones to work their magic, and to prepare myself mentally. Being a woman was complicated. To pass in public, I still needed to wear a wig and a push-up bra. I was also getting laser hair removal of my beard, but I still needed to use heavy foundation and powder to hide the beard shadow.

For many years in my teaching career, I recognized students who showed signs of gender expression that crossed the gender divide. While I had a special place in my heart for these students, I felt like I could not be a role model for them without outing myself. Still, I did my best to be supportive and to build bridges to them. Where I currently teach is the first school I have worked for that has a Gay-Straight Alliance (GSA) club, and students are much more open and free to express their true selves. One of my students revealed to me, in front of classmates, that she considers herself to be *gender fluid*, a term that was new to me. She had short hair and often wore masculine clothes, though she presented a more feminine side at times. I love the concept of being gender fluid, though I see myself as fitting more into the gender binary, just on the opposite side from where I was assigned at birth.

In my current job, I directed two school plays in my first year, and I talked my gender-fluid student into auditioning. While directing my first play, I saw how difficult it was to get boys to audition, and I ended up with quite a few girls. I asked my student if she would be willing to take on a male role, and she agreed. Another student, one of the few boys who performed in both plays, demonstrated openness in expressing femininity. Whenever I had students go into the costume closet and pick out something, he always went for a dress and put it on. In an improvisation exercise he chose to walk and move like a girl. These two students seemed unafraid of nonconforming gender expression, which left me feeling a little more hopeful.

One day I walked into the room of a colleague who was the faculty advisor for the GSA club. I said, "Since you run the GSA club, I was wondering what you see in terms of the atmosphere around campus toward our LGBT students."

She told me that the community is fairly conservative, but the school administration, as well as quite a few of the faculty, supports the GSA club. Some parents, she said, have complained about the club, but the administration always handles it and keeps her fairly isolated from the negativity.

Then I asked, "What about transgender?"

She told me that she knew of a few students who were transgender, and one had actually started to transition, but only after moving to a different school.

I asked her if she knew about the transgender support group in a nearby city, and then I revealed to her that I was a current member of that group. She expressed joy that I would be so supportive of LGBT people, and then our time was cut short when students began to enter for the next class.

Later on I received a text from her, offering to continue our conversation via her personal e-mail. I wrote her a long e-mail telling her my story and also my misgivings about whether to stay with teaching in our district, or even at all. I had not heard of a high school teacher who transitioned on the job without facing a barrage of cruelty from teenagers, bile from frightened parents, and icy shoulders from faculty and staff. She and I became close after that, and she gave me some of the best advice I have gotten in my teaching career. She said that kids say and do all sorts of things that are more about their own level of misunderstanding and discomfort, and usually have little to do with the perceived target of the comment or action. Students had at times made not-so-nice comments toward her, but she did not take it personally. Such advice was not really telling me something I did not already know, but it helped me put things in perspective. When you are in the moment, emotion takes over. The difference between her and me, though, was that she was comfortable with who she was and I was not. She said that, regardless of how people react, it would likely not affect me as much if I was living as my true self, and eventually my transition would be old news.

My colleague also revealed to me that she had heard nothing but positive comments about me from students, which is unusual, since they often like to complain about teachers behind their backs. On top of that, she pointed out that this was my first year at a school with a tightly knit community, and it usually takes at least a couple of years for a new teacher to win approval from the student body. It was hard for me to believe, given that I often saw a different picture when students were in front of me, but soon I began to see more evidence. Other staff started to mention how much students appreciated me. My department head told me that kids told him that they like how I teach, and that they have learned a great deal in my classes.

On the last day of classes, one of my students wrote "We ♥ U" on my board. When I was alone in my room, getting things stored away for the summer, I stared at that statement for a long time. Just months earlier, I was thinking about ending my life, and here, right in front of me, was the best reason why I should vanquish all negative thoughts from my mind. I wept, looking at that statement. Throughout my last few days in my room before break, I kept it on my board. Erasing it was the last thing I did before I left.

I still do not know how my transition will play out in my district. I have at least one ally at work, and I will build more support. If my students really do love me, they will learn to adjust, as will faculty and administration. And maybe even parents, in time. While there is still uncertainty, there is also hope. I just have to have faith in myself and keep moving forward.

21

Questions to Self: Being a
Queer Latino Educator

Benny Vásquez

DIRECTOR OF DIVERSITY

New York, New York

I stood outside and adjusted my tie right before I walked in. This was only the second time I had visited this classroom and I wanted to make an impression. I held my *And Tango Makes Three* book closely to my chest and realized that my hands had left a slightly wet mark on the plastic cover. I breathed and asked myself, "Why am I so nervous?" I took a moment to gather my breath: I wiped my hands on my pressed linen pants and walked into the classroom.

It was the first time I had ever read a book that focused on anything gay, and I wasn't sure how it was going to be received. I was asked by the teacher to come in and read a book that provided a space to talk about different families, specifically gay families. A student, who happened to have two gay dads, was feeling picked on and felt that no one understood where he was coming from. As the director of diversity, I was often looked at to start these types of conversations. So, I did.

All the second-grade eyes were looking at me. Their eyes beamed with excitement at a new visitor. The students hardly knew me yet were quick in welcoming me into their space. Their smiles made me feel slightly at ease. I stepped inside the classroom and was surprised to hear the symphony of greetings—"*Buenos días!*" "Good morning," and "Hi, Mr. Vásquez!"—all sounding like the thirty seconds you spend in the car switching radio stations, hearing different songs and waiting to hear the right sound that would allow you to survive the traffic jam. I took it all in. I looked around and noticed the posters of Martin Luther King Jr., Dolores Huerta, and one with the Gandhi quote "Be the change you want to see in the world." These three figures had always been a part of my life and my pedagogy, and looking at them at this moment felt like a sign. I told myself, "You got this," sat down, and prepared myself for opening the meeting. The kids rushed to the carpet, formed a circle, and had all their eyes on the book I was holding in my hand.

I opened my book and began to read. As I read the story of the two male penguins raising a baby penguin named Tango in Central Park, students raised their hands in excitement and simultaneously let me know that they too had been to the Central Park Zoo. Their commentary allowed me to laugh and feel more at ease with the rest of the story. As I read, I noticed my breath getting calmer as I began to enjoy the story. It was amazing to see their eyes as they attempted to make sense of the fact that love exists in different ways—even between "two boy penguins," as one student proclaimed. As the story came to its end I noticed Jonathan, the boy with two dads, sitting across from me and hanging on my every word. He was smiling, with eyes wide open, and seemed to be excited to hear an aspect of his story being told.

I finished and answered some simple questions ranging from "How is Tango now?" "Can I go see Tango at Central Park?" "Can penguins live in the beach?" and "How old are Tango's parents?" The questions came rapid-fire, but I was able to answer all of them with ease. That all changed when I called on Jonathan. He quickly asked three questions all at once: "Are you married? Are you gay like Tango's parents? Do you have kids?" My heart stopped. All twenty-two sets of eyes were on me, waiting for my response. In my head all these questions appeared at once. *What do I say? Do I lie? I need to pay my rent!* My heart started beating rapidly, and I looked at him and said, "Yes, I am married to a man and, just like Tango's parents, I am starting a family." Students just looked at me and smiled. As I was about to continue talking, Jonathan interrupted and talked about his two dads and their trip to the zoo, which allowed other students to chime in and make a connection. I looked at the clock and realized it was time for me to go. I quickly got up, thanked them, and continued to my next meeting,

I had been in the role of director of diversity at this school for only one month, and I felt excited that I could have these conversations within the school. As I walked down the hall, I felt a sense of accomplishment. As a queer Latino male, it had been rare to feel I could walk into a space and just be. As an educator, I always hesitated to show my true self. I never had a picture of Miguel on my office desk. I always avoided answering the question from kids, "Mr. Vasquez, are you married?" or "Do you have a girlfriend?" Yet I often was very vocal when my gay white colleagues would ask me the flippant question "Why are black people so homophobic?" while not understanding that that question in itself screams "*Stereotype!*"

Many times I felt as if I led a triple life. One was my *queer, out, activist, Latino self*, who holds up a protest sign at the drop of a hat. My second was my *work self*, one who was out with fellow teachers. I was the one who would push conversations about LGBT rights in our workspace, stressing the need for gender-inclusive language and a diverse curriculum that went beyond Harvey Milk. My third was rather different. That third self was me as *a teacher*. I was constantly fearful that I would be asked a question about my sexuality. I didn't fear the reaction of the students but rather the reaction of the institution under which I was working. Although I know that getting fired for one's sexuality is illegal in New York State and *so* 1980s (at least in New York City's independent schools), I still wanted to keep this part of my life outside the classroom. I was comfortable with fellow straight teachers sharing their stories with students about their weddings, what they had done that weekend, or having their significant other pick them up from work. But for me, I felt more comfortable staying in the closet. What if I said the wrong thing? What if I were to get fired for saying, "No, I don't have a wife. I have a husband!"? What if I am accused of being inappropriate? I often think of where

this unfounded fear comes from. Is it my internalized homophobia? Have I been trained to constantly be in a state of awareness and
doubt? Probably so.

As I was answering Jonathan's questions, these thoughts came
into my head, but I decided to let them go. I decided to see what happens and be free of the doubt and be my true self.

After that second-grade visit, I felt alive. I felt whole. I felt that
I came out again, and this time it was easy. All those doubts began
to disappear. I was confident that I had used all my skills to answer
questions while remaining "appropriate." Days passed and I was on
a high.

When I entered the cafeteria a week later my high quickly dis-
sipated. As I was getting my coffee, a parent approached me and
sternly demanded to talk to me. Her tone was odd and I was unsure of
what was to follow. She began to tell me in a firm voice that—and I
quote—"Saying the word *gay* is a bad word in my house, and I would
hope you never say it again!" Her voice was stern, angry, and without
an ounce of shame. As she continued her tirade, I began to feel my
heart beat faster, my breath shorten. The cafeteria was empty. The
sounds of the NYC traffic had muted and all that was left was her
voice and her anger. I quickly woke up, fixed my perplexed look, and
began to formulate a sentence that could serve as a response, one
that could soothe her anger and get me out of the situation as quickly
as possible. I began to tell her the importance of using language that
is inclusive and that prepared our children to interact with "different" types of people. I stressed the need for us to accept people for
who they are, no matter *what* they are. She looked at me with displeasure and got up. She left me midsentence as I was talking about the
importance of language and acceptance. She walked out and didn't
look back.

I looked on as she walked out of the cafeteria. Her body was
tensed up and her hands were clenched. She stomped up the stairs,
leaving the sound of her feet lingering in the background and filling
the empty space. I looked around. I was the only one there, the only
one to take in this news, the only one to respond, the only one to

make sense of what had just happened. I got up, went to my office, closed my door, and cried.

That was almost five years ago, and her voice—the voice of bigotry—still haunts me. Although I have moved on and realize that this is the work I have to do as a Queer Latino Educator, that voice continues to instill me with fear and the sense that I am doing something wrong. Every day I fight to get rid of that voice. I fight to make sure that I can be whoever I am. I fight for inclusive spaces, to continue providing examples, not only for Jonathan but also for all the students who are in the classroom and wanting to know if it's okay to love who they love.

I have accepted that I am a Queer Latino Educator. I am a Queer Latino Educator—one who will use his voice for the work that needs to be undone and the work that needs to be done. I am a Queer Latino Educator—one who will introduce his students and school community to the power of inclusivity and language. I am a Queer Latino Educator—one who lives with three selves and is working to make them one. I am a Queer Latino Educator—one who will teach, love, and strive to be who he is and to create spaces where people don't want me to hide. I am a Queer Latino Educator—one who will work to make sure that we have schools that aim to create spaces where all our identities can enter. I am a Queer Latino Educator.

22

We're Not Nearly There

Duran Renkema

TEACHER GROUP 8 PRIMARY SCHOOL
CSG De Waard
Rotterdam, Holland

My name is Duran Renkema. I am a forty-six-year-old teacher living in Rotterdam, Holland, with my husband, Ton te Riele.

Holland is known for its tolerance and its gay-friendly climate. And yet, when I came out as gay in 2011, my employer tried to dump me not because of who I was but because of what I was. I fought back and became the center of a national media circus that lasted for more than eighteen months.

I was born in 1967 into a loving family. I grew up in a small town in Holland with my brother and my younger sister. My parents were devoted Christians, and the church we went to was very conservative. It preached love and happiness to the ones who followed the rules, and hell, death, and despair to the ones who wandered off. Love was a thin varnish that hid a darker, self-centered community. Every Sunday we would hear the long list of sinners. Gays and other "sexual abominations" were always part of that list. It was clear to me: gays go to hell. My mind was made up about homosexuality even before knowing the concept of sexual orientation, let alone knowing what mine was.

As a teenager, I learned that I was different. I did like girls, sure. But there was something about boys too. It didn't take me long to realize I must be more or less bisexual. It wasn't even a big shock to me, but I realized that other people would not feel the same way. The church was involved in every little part of our lives—Sundays, but every other day of the week too. School, friends, family . . . all part of the same church, all part of the same narrow-minded and loveless community I knew so well. Coming out as bisexual was no option. The idea of becoming an abomination was so frightening that I instantly decided that this was a part of me I would have to hide forever. And so I did, and quite successfully too. I became a guy with a mask, hiding the part of me that would never be accepted or loved by the people who surrounded me.

Having two dreams, working in education and working as a graphic designer, I chose the latter when I was eighteen. I finished art school, moved out of my parents' house, and started working in the advertising business as a junior designer. I liked the job and it paid the bills.

I became an active church member, taking part in many church subgroups and commissions. I was part of the church band and conductor of the choir. But as I got in deeper and deeper, I became depressed and unhappy. Not wanting to break the image of Mr. Perfect I had created, this truth about my bisexuality was something that had to disappear behind the mask as well. And it did. I managed to survive like this for several years.

After a few disappointing love affairs, I met Mary in 1994. There was an instant click, and not long after we started dating we decided to get married. Apart from the fact that we were fond of each other, marriage, I thought, was the perfect way to get rid of my masked past once and for all. We got married one year later, and for the first time in my life I felt truly free and happy. We had a few very good years, with a daughter being born in 1997 and a son in 2000. I worked my way up in the advertising business into management, and by then I made enough money for us to have a very nice life. I worked twelve hours a day, and we moved to a new, big house and thought we had it all. We never even noticed the dark clouds gathering above our heads.

In 2001 Mary was diagnosed with multiple sclerosis. The future we had planned so well vanished into thin air. We were devastated, not knowing what tomorrow was going to bring. We made some big decisions that year. To us, money, status, and luxury lost their meaning completely. Knowing Mary would end up in a wheelchair sooner or later, I decided to quit my job and go for a job as a schoolteacher. Not only was that one of my early dreams, but more important, it gave me more time and freedom to take care of Mary and the kids. A member of our church was in charge of a large group of highly traditional Christian schools in Holland (GPO-WN), and he asked me to join his organization. After I finished a three-year course of study successfully, I started working there as a teacher in September 2004.

As Mary's situation got worse, I worked harder and harder and became both father and mother to our two young children. Mary needed help with most everyday things like showers and getting dressed. In the next couple of years my work around the house expanded, and together with my full-time job at school I became a machine that kept our family going, with no time left to socialize or relax. As Mary was obviously always the center of attention, I disappeared completely into the background. Regarding her illness and the way people around her put constant focus on her situation, Mary changed too. If there was one thing people around us had taught her, it was that life was about her. Without even noticing it, she became more and more self-centered, quite the opposite of the woman I married.

While Mary went through changes of her own, so did I. I became more and more unsatisfied with the role I'd been given. I wanted my life back, instead of being the motor of someone else's. Slowly but surely we drifted apart, which resulted in many arguments, high tension, and eventually four unhappy people. Our once-happy marriage was long gone. We were merely putting up with each other, and an overdose of guilt, responsibility, and fear of change was the glue that kept us together.

Then I met Ton. Each of us was attending a mutual friend's party on our own, and it didn't take long for our eyes to meet. Lightning struck. Every wall I built, every fence I put up collapsed in one single moment. This was me, there was no escape. And I didn't want to either. We talked for a long time and exchanged phone numbers.

We met on several other occasions, and I knew that this was what I wanted, what I had been longing for all my life. Everything fell into place. I didn't care if I was an abomination anymore; this was the way I was born to be. It's like being locked and raised inside a room with drawn curtains, and then suddenly, after forty-four years, someone walks in and opens every window. The view is so wide and breathtaking, you can't imagine how you've managed to live without it for so long. I wanted only one thing, and that was being close to Ton for the rest of my life.

Of course I knew that coming out as gay would have some nasty effects. Not only would my marriage end, but I would also get into trouble with the church, my employer, and my family. Although the general opinion about homosexuality changed slightly in some religious areas, our church was certainly not in one of those areas and I'd probably be thrown out instantly, regardless of how much time and effort I had put into the church in the past twenty years.

My employer would probably raise an eyebrow and have a firm conversation with me, but I expected them to understand on some level.

But what about my family? My parents, brother, sister, in-laws? All part of the same church in the same town . . . I had seen before how differences like these could tear up families for good and isolate the "sinners." I was scared like hell that something like that would happen to me after I came out.

Scared or not, it was something I had to do. No turning back, no more masks. On the evening of April 24, 2011, I decided to close my eyes and jump.

It was even worse than I had imagined. Coming out to Mary has been one of the most horrible experiences I have ever gone through. I will carry it with me for as long as I live. The guilt I felt was almost unbearable. I left the house in a hurry that night, as Mary called her family for support and I did not want to get lynched by an angry mob. I went to Ton's place. He lived in Rotterdam, about sixty miles from where we lived. In the car I kept repeating to myself, "There's no turning back now, there's no turning back now . . ." During that frantic ride I got text messages from Mary's family with all kinds of threats and horrible imprecations.

The next day I returned to Mary, as we had decided that we should tell the kids together. They were in tears, of course, and Mary kept yelling, "See what you're doing to them? See what you're doing to them?" Eventually she left with the kids and went to her mother, who lived a few blocks away. I went to see my parents, sister, and brother to tell them what had happened, only to learn that my mother-in-law had already informed everyone they knew—including my mother—about me. Their hate spreading would go on for a long time after that day.

My fear that my parents would turn a cold shoulder was proven wrong, and although both were worried about what the future would bring for me, they embraced me with love, as did my sister. My brother's reaction was colder. After I talked to him we didn't see or speak to each other for almost three years.

Most of our close friends felt they needed to choose sides and teamed up with Mary, who obviously needed a lot of support then. I didn't blame them, but felt very much alone. These friends whom I had always been there for and who were so precious to me turned a cold shoulder, and I was put on "ignore mode." I never heard from them again.

That day I also informed my employer GPO-WN by e-mail about the things that had happened in our private lives and asked for one day off to get things on track again for myself. A reply came almost instantly: they were unpleasantly surprised and I was not welcome anymore. They would think about what actions they would take against me. I was invited to a meeting with them and their lawyers the next week.

I could not believe that my sexual orientation and choice of partner would be reason for them to get rid of me, and after a few days of feeling sad and confused, I decided to fight back.

With help from Ton and some friends in Rotterdam, I asked for assistance from COC (the Dutch LGBT organization), Company Pride Platform, and some other people. With a large LGBT network we contacted several law firms. A big Dutch law firm, Kennedy Van Der Laan, offered their help for free.

We had a meeting with the board of directors of GPO-WN and their lawyers, in which the organization stated literally that because of my homosexual orientation they did not wish to have anything to do with me anymore, as I was clearly not fit to teach children, having such low morals.

They bluntly offered me a very small sum of money if I would agree to leave silently. Of course I refused, and after three hours the meeting ended with no result.

Then GPO-WN started a lawsuit. Dutch law protects people against discrimination by way of the Equal Treatment Law, and you can't be fired just because you're gay. However, in 1994 the government added a special article to the Equal Treatment Law. Translated, it was called the Sole Fact Construction (SFC). It provided orthodox religious employers in the educational field with the unique ability of getting rid of gay teachers and students if they could provide additional and special circumstances that would justify it. The nature of those circumstances wasn't mentioned, and thus a large gray area was created.

GPO-WN used the SFC to justify my removal from their organization.

My lawyers and I decided that we would ask the Dutch Committee for Equal Treatment for a judgment on this matter. Their judgment would be leading in the lawsuit.

From the moment we did so (September 29, 2011), the case went public and things exploded. Television, radio, journalists from all the national newspapers and magazines called and wanted to talk. It turned out that until now nobody in the Netherlands had ever fought back when fired on these grounds.

In twenty-four hours Ton and I went from invisible to Twitter's trending topic, and we were all over the news. The phone didn't stop ringing, everybody seemed to aim at an interview, and we were invited to major national television talk shows.

COC handled most of these media requests, as this was the last thing on our minds. Ton and I just wanted to be left alone when we had so much to consider and think about.

In the past few months the relationship with Mary and the kids had been going very well, as we all realized that what had happened was inevitable and ultimately for the better. Although a separation is always a sad thing for everyone involved, we managed to remain friends. Without the tension of living together, communication between us seemed to improve. Ton and I kept Mary and the kids informed of every decision that was made, and it was a relief when she said she was behind us all the way. This turned out to be extremely important, as people from GPO-WN's circle had a nasty surprise waiting for us.

While the date of the trial, which was set for October 14, was getting closer, it seemed obvious that we would win the case. As GPO-WN knew that, they changed their strategy completely. They changed their law firm and decided to work with a Christian law firm with a nasty reputation. This law firm was known for their way of destroying people and reputations. As long as they won, it didn't seem to matter how they got there. What they thought the Bible said was more important to them than what the law said.

Their new strategy included a nasty media plan. My reputation was to be destroyed. If they could succeed in making me look like a selfish and bad person who didn't care about his sick wife and poor children, then that might change the way things seemed to be going. With the help of some Christian newspapers and people who worked at evangelical radio and TV companies, some nasty rumors were spread. Suddenly my wife and children were pushed to the front line, with pictures and sad, made-up stories of how this adulterer ruined the life of his family to pursue his own pleasures, leaving them helpless and with no money. A Dutch TV evangelist did some interviews in which he implied he was an insider on the matter. He told people I had been cheating on my wife for ages, and that was the reason GPO-WN wanted to get rid of me. Surely this could not be tolerated as an example for the kids at my school. I had "low morals" and the world needed to know. I didn't even know the guy but found out he had links with GPO-WN.

The lies and stories that popped up in the media were appalling, and many orthodox Christian people felt the need to send nasty messages and threats to my Facebook and Twitter accounts, believing every word they were fed by the Christian media.

Also, politicians from two traditional Christian parties in Holland started their own little war on homosexuality and on me in particular, stating that freedom of religion was more important than the right to be who you are. I was portrayed as the man who was the enemy of religion and Christian schools. These two politicians also had their links with GPO-WN, and it became crystal clear the other side was working hard to get what they wanted.

A local church showed my picture at the beginning of the service, and the preacher told the people, "This is what's wrong with the world. This is your enemy!" My aunt was in that church and left crying.

I talked about it with Mary, who was obviously not amused with the sudden attention on her and the children. We never wanted this to happen, and we thought about ways to stop it.

We decided to write an open letter together to the main Dutch newspapers and TV and radio companies. In this letter we distanced ourselves from all the nasty things that were written about us, and we made a clear statement that these people obviously knew nothing about us and they should refrain from lies and rumor spreading. Our breakup was our private business, and this public attack was clearly meant to take the focus off the true heart of the case: discrimination because of sexual orientation. We signed the letter together.

The letter was published in newspapers and on the Internet, and several radio shows mentioned it. I also placed it on the front page of my own website. After this, things calmed down a bit. Of course, the Christian newspapers and media kept shooting their arrows at us, as we were clearly "pure evil."

On October 14 we had our first and only hearing at the court. Mary, Ton, and I traveled together and went into the building as fast as we could. My parents were there and some friends too, as well as people from COC and other LGBT organizations.

The hearing itself was fairly predictable. When GPO-WN tried to convince the judge that the whole thing had nothing to do with my sexual orientation but everything to do with my low moral standards (adulterer, bad father, bad husband, bad Christian), we presented the court with an audio recording of the first meeting. Ton had cleverly recorded the whole thing on his iPad. Originally meant for our own use, to listen to it again when we would come home after a confusing day, it was now evidence that GPO-WN was manipulative and had been lying.

Soon after presenting this evidence, the hearing ended and we all went home.

In the two weeks after the hearing there were a couple of interviews, some articles in the media, but apart from that, things quieted down. Thank God.

We got an e-mail from the church. They obviously wanted to officially exclude me from the church. As the director of GPO-WN also was the head of the church board, I wasn't surprised, and I tried not to care. But it does hurt when after twenty years of loyalty you get dumped like trash.

On November 2, 2011, the verdict of the court was made public. I got a call from our lawyer. We had won. Big time. We talked a long time as our lawyer explained the verdict.

The court decided that my employer had no right whatsoever to fire me as I had a perfect service record. They decided that GPO-WN was discriminating against me and its actions were against the law. My employer had shown bad judgment by not offering me the chance for an honest discussion about the possibilities of continuing my work at GPO-WN.

A weight had been lifted off my shoulders. I was still holding my phone when the doorbell rang and people came in to congratulate me. It was all over the news.

Journalists called and showed up at the door, TV interviews were recorded. . . . I can't say I remember all that happened that day. It was so frantic, I had difficulties focusing on everything.

The next day GPO-WN made a sour comment on their website that "they respected the verdict of the court, but were very disappointed and would find it very difficult to show respect to me when they were forced into another meeting with us."

They were forced into that meeting, as the court ruled that we had to talk again about my continuing working at GPO-WN. Two weeks later that meeting took place, but it was obvious they didn't want me back and would do everything in their power to make life miserable for me at work.

We decided not to go through the whole thing again. We got what we wanted: the court was on our side, and my employer was proven wrong in front of the whole country. So we decided to let it go and look to the future.

I had already received offers from various schools in the Rotterdam area that had followed the whole thing in the media, and I accepted one of them. On January 2 I was officially employed with another school, and finally got the time and peace to digest it all and focus on my future.

It's been three years now.

On various occasions I was invited to be a guest on TV talk shows when the subject involved sexuality, religion, and education. I helped other people who were in the same position I was. I worked hard to help improve the position of gay brothers and sisters in a religious environment.

I taught people, but I learned a lot too. I learned a lot of Christian people aren't as hateful as the fanatics. In fact, many are very caring and loving. I learned to avoid prejudice, and by overcoming that I could try and make other people do the same.

Ton and I got married in the summer of 2013. Surrounded by hundreds of (new) friends, colleagues, our parents, and my sister, we made our love official with a firm "I do." I can honestly say that it was one of the happiest days of my life.

My case was exactly what some pro-LGBT politicians needed in order to get the SFC clause removed from the law, which was done only in 2014. Again this caused some commotion, accompanied by a flurry of media attention.

Now, finally, Dutch laws truly protect the rights of gay teachers and students. Never again can someone's sexual orientation in the Netherlands be cause for firing a teacher or dismissing a student. Our case sent out a strong signal: we're all equal and should be treated like equals.

Even in Holland we still have a lot to fight for. Even here some people still believe we are sick and need to be healed. I feel tolerated most of the time, but many times I feel far from accepted.

I will keep on fighting for what I believe in.

We're not nearly there.

Epilogue: Polishing Up Our Schools

Rodney Glasgow

HEAD OF MIDDLE SCHOOL AND CHIEF DIVERSITY OFFICER
St. Andrew's Episcopal School
Potomac, Maryland

I'm sitting in my office and the last bell has just rung. As is usual at this time of day, my office explodes with the energy of middle schoolers. One student has come in with a Tupperware of supplies. She noticed that it's been a while since my nails were painted, and she has graciously offered to spend time playing nail shop while we catch up on our day. When she asked me a few days earlier, I could tell it took all the courage in the world for her to say, "You know, I'd really like to paint your nails. Could I?" I knew it was less about my raggedy cuticles and more about finding a way to connect with me. When a middle schooler invites you to connect, you accept!

As she's laying out her various colors and making small talk, several of the boys drift in to say hello. "What are you doing?" they ask my young stylist. "I'm painting Mr. Glasgow's nails." "Oh, cool. Can we pick the color? Mr. Glasgow, what do you think of pink?" "I'll wear whatever color you pick out for me," I say. "Just don't make me look busted!" They pick a glow-in-the-dark pink, of course, and stay to chat through the application process, talking about their school day, who wants to date whom, and their eagerness to get to high school. With my left hand halfway done, one of the school chaplains comes by to talk about next week's chapel. She sits in the rocking chair in the corner of my office, kids spread out all around, and joins the conversation for a few minutes. Now with my left hand looking a gorgeous light pink and my right hand ready for color, three boys and two girls, just returning from a conference for students of color, come bursting through the door, eager to share their day with me. They think nothing of the crowd in the office, or the painted nails. It all makes sense to them.

Having beautiful nails is hard work. Fifteen years ago when I reported for work at my first independent school, my painted nails were the talk of the town, but more like disapproving whispers and not so well hidden sneers. I was a very different person than that school was accustomed to. My differences, represented in my nail color and skin color, became a point of departure for me with the parent community. They were so worried that their children might develop a new sense of normal. I could have avoided a lot of conflict with a bottle of acetone and a strong handshake. But my authenticity resonated with students, and they found solace and joy in connecting with an adult who wasn't afraid to be himself. It made them feel safe, which in turn, made them feel brave. My office was a welcomed shelter from the need to conform.

I knew I was not safe when my manicured hand pulled an anonymous note out of my school mailbox. It had a picture of an old Jim Crow caricature with the word *nigger* typed across it and a message that said, "We thought this would make you feel at home, fag." Shocked, panic-stricken, I assumed that the letter came from a group of anonymous parents. Adding black to gay to gender nonconforming at that time netted negative. Because self-determination about when and how I enter and exit a space is one of my core principles, I stayed at that school for three years. But I refused to do crossing-guard duty, as a stop sign seemed an insufficient barrier between me and misplaced aggression.

I think about that school as the student puts the finishing touches on my nails and students head to the circle for pickup. I sit at my desk, hands spread out strategically on the desktop to prevent any accidents in the drying process. I observe my manicured hands, and while I wait for them to dry, I smile pensively. Progress is a beautiful thing. Now, my nails are still a conversation piece, but it's more about how the color looks with my skin tone. The student's mother thanks me the next day for spending that time with her daughter, who told her about it with great excitement the evening before. Fifteen years ago, I would not have thought this level of comfort around difference was possible in my elite private-school world. There is still room for progress, but there is no doubt that schools are becoming safer places. Every day, I am blessed to go to work in a place where authenticity needs no apology. That's a good thing, because my mom taught me never to apologize unless I had something to apologize for.

Acknowledgments

The first person I have to thank is a contributor to this volume, Erika Cobain. Erika (whom I did not know) e-mailed me out of the blue in early 2014 and suggested I do a third volume of this anthology. Her suggestion prompted its creation. Thanks for pushing me, Erika!

The team at Beacon Press deserve enormous credit as well. First, Helene Atwan enthusiastically embraced the project and then gave me the privilege of working with Alexis Rizzuto and Will Myers, who were extraordinary partners in creating this book and championing it. I am particularly grateful for their sharp editorial eyes. They have been an absolute pleasure to work with.

Some other folks did behind-the-scenes work that made this book immeasurably stronger, including Stephanie Wade, whose admin support caught many details I would have missed; Sharon Lettman-Hicks of the National Black Justice Coalition, whose personal outreach to African American educators helped diversify the collection; and Jacob Huang of Aibai, who not only identified Chinese contributors but also translated their submissions so that I could actually read them. Thank you all.

I am blessed with an incredible circle of supportive family and friends, and it would be impossible for me to thank all of them, so thanking any makes me nervous as I fear someone's feelings will be hurt by being left out. But two women have to get called out. The first is Christie Hardwick, whose wisdom and guidance have been invaluable to me for nearly fifteen years. The second is my "fairy godmother" (I'm the fairy; she's the godmother), Graciela Kaplan, who adopted me nearly a quarter of a century ago and has been my rock ever since. I love you both more than you can imagine.

Finally, I have to give the biggest heaping of credit to my partner, Jeff Davis. Ironically, we met on December 1, 1994, when he came to a reading of the first edition of *One Teacher in Ten* in New York, so I literally would not have him in my life without this ongoing project. Nothing I have accomplished since would have been possible without his love and support. You complete me.

Oh, and by the way, the right answer is Wisconsin.